AMERICAN MUSCLE

MUSCLE CARS FROM THE OTIS CHANDLER COLLECTION

Randy Leffingwell

Motorbooks International
Publishers & Wholesalers ®

This book is dedicated to Richard Hinson and Wallace D. Guenther

First published in 1990 by Motorbooks International Publishers & Wholesalers, P O Box 2, 729 Prospect Avenue, Osceola, WI 54020 USA

Motorbooks International books are also available at discounts in bulk quantity for industrial or sales-promotional use. For details write to Special Sales Manager at the Publisher's address

Library of Congress Cataloging-in-Publication Data
Leffingwell, Randy.
    American muscle / Randy Leffingwell.
        p. cm.
    ISBN 0-87938-465-4
    1. Muscle cars—United States—History.   I. Title.
TL23.L37   1990   90-35906
629.222—dc20   CIP

Printed and bound in Singapore by PH Productions

On the front cover: *The 1969 Chevrolet Camaro Baldwin Motion Phase III. Modified by Motion Performance and sold through Baldwin Chevrolet on Long Island, New York, the Phase III Camaro produced 500 hp and would turn the quarter-mile in 11.4 sec. at 120 mph.*

On the back cover: *The last Hemi 'Cuda ever built, May 19, 1971. In six years of production, only 159 Hemi convertibles were constructed and sold, including seven in 1971. It was the end of an era.*

On the frontispiece: *The 1970 Pink Panther Plymouth 'Cuda Hemi coupe: 426 ci, 425 hp.*

On the title page: *The 1969 Dodge Coronet R/T Hemi convertible. One great beach cruiser, this four-speed Hemi was a surprisingly nimble handling car—and it was still large enough for four serious surfers and long boards.*

On the last page: *The Hemi 'Cuda Shaker hood in action.*

Contents

Acknowledgments

As everyone who writes one knows, a book is not merely the work of its author alone. It is the combined effort of many people, their generous help and accommodation, that made this work.

First, my sincere thanks to Otis and Bettina Chandler. Without Otis' perception, foresight and enthusiasm, the collection would not exist. The Chandlers' kindness and generosity to me in making available these cars, their time and their extensive research library made this work the greatest pleasure.

My thanks to Ron Hussey, Anne Proffit and Don Burgess for the germination of this idea.

So many people provided locations, suggestions, ideas and assistance. I am grateful to you all: Alan and Lin Ayers, The Ayers Pumpkin Patch on Faulkner Farm, Santa Paula, California; Colleen Bailey, Los Angeles County Raceway; Bill Brensel, Quinn Company Caterpillar, Oxnard, California; Larry Calderon and Paul Jacobs at Oxnard College Warehouses; Pete Canbier and Tom Sonneman at California Bean Growers Association; Lieutenant Colonel Myron B. Carpenter, Jr., and the 146th Tactical Airlift Wing, Channel Islands California Air National Guard; Carmen Chappell, Ventura County Rail Road; Sean Chung, Angelo's Drive In Hamburgers, Anaheim, California; Paul W. Crook, Chevrolet-Pontiac-Canada Group, General Motors, Van Nuys, California; Don Dalbey, CALTRANS; Mary Duncan, Gold's Gym, Oxnard; Dr. Paris Earls, Newbury Park High School; Joe Esparza and the Alfred Hartman Ranches; John Falk at Sycamore Cove State Beach; Greg and Pat Garrison; Bob Harmuth, Port Hueneme Harbor; Judy Harpster, Limoneira Associates, Santa Paula; Mattie Henderson, Planning Department, City of Pasadena; Bob Hubbert, Pacific Missile Test Center, US Navy, Point Mugu; Lieutenant Stan Jacobsen, Pacific Missile Test Center; John Jensen, Ventura County Sheriff Department; Bill Legan, Ventura County Fire Department; Sue Little and Betze Snead, Riverside International Raceway; Dave Long; Phil Lukens, Blair's Speed Shop, Pasadena; Chuck Maslin; Jerry Menesez; Martin Menne, SAMMIS-Del Norte Associates, Oxnard; Vern and Ed Savko; Dan Schenk, Super Shops, Oxnard; Randell K. Taylor, Pasadena Police Department Special Event Planning Unit; Don and Susan Tholander; Jim Utter, California Highway Patrol; Tom Vujovich; Chuck and Nancy Willhite, Newbury Park, California.

Technical thanks go to everyone at A&I, Los Angeles; Irwin Buxbaum at Lee-Mac Cameras, Pasadena; Armando Flores at Nikon Professional Services; and Steve Rahm at Samy's Camera, Los Angeles.

Special thanks go to Larry Armstrong, Bob Chamberlin and Cindy Hively on the photo assignment desk at the *Los Angeles Times* for every consideration imaginable and for their patience and tolerance.

I owe Leslie Evans at the Vintage Museum and Mary LaBarre at Motorbooks bundles of roses for their help.

To Zora Arkus-Duntov, Bob Cahill, Jack Cheskaty, John Clinard, Lynn Ferguson, Tom Hoover, Tom Hoxie, Marvin Hughes, Dave Long, Paul Preuss, Larry Rathgeb, Gary Romberg, Joel Rosen, Wayne Scraba, Carroll Shelby and the Society of Automotive Engineers, who generously gave of their time and memories, please know that this book is much the better for your help. Thank you.

Thanks to Ford Motor Company and the Society of Automotive Engineers for permission to reprint portions of SAE report 611F, *The Mustang, Ford's Experimental Sports Car*, by Roy Lunn. And also thanks to Anthony Young for permission to quote from his book *Mighty Mopars 1960–1974*, published by Motorbooks International.

Greg Joseph and Michael Dregni assisted tremendously in making me correct and literate.

I am grateful to Steve and Christie McAvoy for their friendship and generous hospitality. Their help made this work seem like a vacation.

I am grateful beyond measure to Jerry Sewell, general manager of the Vintage Museum, and to his wife, Lisa, and children, Staci and Josh. Jerry's enthusiasm and wisdom were an immense contribution to this book. His understanding of my location desires and his willingness to work preposterously long days (and nights) without complaint became a key to the photography of this book.

To you all, my thanks.

Randy Leffingwell
Los Angeles, California

Randy Leffingwell is a staff photographer and writer for the *Los Angeles Times*.

Preface

Cars and speed have always been a passion of mine . . . and still are.

I can't quite remember where or why I first knew they would be a dominant force in my life. I guess it was my first homemade go-cart I fabricated from my dad's discarded old power mower.

Since I was shipped off to an eastern prep school for high school, I missed all the good stuff . . . street rods, low riders, drags. In fact, my first power vehicle was a big red 1948 Harley 74, which was my college wheels until my senior year when I sprung for a beat-up but drivable five-window Ford coupe. From that moment on I was hooked on cars, motorcycles, later race cars and definitely speed!

Next came marriage, an air force hitch and five children, and, ugh, years of station wagons. I followed the muscle cars: occasional trips with good friend Mickey Thompson to the drags. Later came a brief period of amateur and professional racing in Porsches and collecting a few great classic cars.

Three years ago the classics and sports and race cars began their upward spiral in price as speculators and heavy-duty new collectors pumped in millions overnight. The hobby I loved disappeared. I sold most of my cars and decided to see if I could be content just to watch.

It didn't last long. I decided one day in 1987 to buy a few muscle cars. They were reasonably cheap, fun to drive, noisy and fast. I met a local college professor, a classic and antique collector, and, most important to me at the time, an absolute muscle car fanatic . . .

he had the knowledge of where to find them and shared my dedication to rarity and documentation and diversity. He also has a computerlike memory of what cars to buy for the museum. At first it was going to be about ten to fifteen. Now we are over fifty with a few more to go—but only if we can find the right ones we need to fill a few missing pieces. Naturally my long-time traditional car collector friends believe I have at last finally gone bananas in my new passion for muscle cars.

And I guess I have . . . in my 1971 Hemi 'Cuda convertible . . . Banana Yellow, natch. Enjoy the collection.

Otis Chandler

Philosophy of the Collection

The initial concept of this collection was born in the spring of 1981. The rigors of graduate school motivated my escape from reality. Instead of mentally agonizing over the historical debate of whether Franklin D. Roosevelt's New Deal program was a radical economic aberration of the past or was steeped in the Progressive reform tradition of the early 1900s, I spent the remainder of one afternoon (and the decade, for that matter!) contemplating the construction of the finest high-performance muscle car collection. I proceeded to devise a list of more than fifty of Detroit's rarest and fastest sixties and early seventies muscle cars. At this point it was nothing more than a burned-out graduate student's wish list. There was never any realistic likelihood of this collection's materializing. Not only would it take a large economic endeavor, but also locating these ultra-rare cars would be next to impossible. I never discarded the original list, however. It became the blueprint for the finest muscle car collection in the world.

The term muscle car means, to borrow a popular political phrase, many things to many people. The emotional debate over this generic term will continue throughout the next generation of car collectors. To avoid further confusion, however, it is important to define the parameters upon which this collection was assembled. Since it is impractical to collect every model made, we have been selective in our choice of cars for the museum.

Muscle cars were Detroit's quarter-mile bombers manufactured in the sixties and early seventies for street and drag strip use. The key here is street *and* strip use—a car street legal yet fast enough to run competitive stock class times at the local drag strip. During this period, the status of American youth was judged by the raw horsepower and cubic inches of their cars. A high-performance car enthusiast could walk into the showroom of the local dealer and fill out a Regular Production Order (RPO) sheet, and possibly drive home with an unbeatable combination. Factory lightweight cars, such as the 1964 Ford Thunderbolt and 1968 Hemi Dodge Dart, were never available to the public. They were all-out factory race cars, not RPO muscle cars. The overall intention of the collection is to acquire only muscle cars intended for public consumption, not for factory drag professionals.

The years between 1960 and 1972 are defined by experts as the apex of American

The Vintage Museum houses Otis Chandler's collection of automobiles dating from the turn of the century to the present day. Covering 45,000 sq ft on two levels, the collection comprises more than 100 vehicles. American muscle cars share space with current super cars. Transportation in its many forms is represented by a narrow-gauge steam locomotive and other unique vehicles including fire trucks and a 1937 Yellowstone Park touring bus. A significant element of the museum is an extensive collection of automotive art. There are several woven tapestries by Los Angeles artist Keith Collins, and designed by Richard Pietruska, bronze sculptures by Stanley Wanlass and Paul Nesse, and original drawings, photographs and paintings.

high-performance muscle cars. Though we acknowledge this interpretation, our emphasis within the collection is the years between 1966 and 1971. This was the period that witnessed the production of the fabled 426 street Hemi, the outrageous L-88 aluminum-head Corvette engine, the beastly ZL-1 aluminum-engine Camaro. Not only was Detroit producing its ultimate powerplants, but each manufacturer had also become dramatically style conscious. Enduro bumpers, front and rear spoilers, and paint and graphic schemes beyond earlier comprehension became the norm among the producers of high-performance

automobiles. Panther Pink, Plum Crazy, Hugger Orange and Lemon Twist Yellow adorned these metal warriors. Raciness in appearance was as important as elapsed-time slips. An individual could order every creature feature imaginable along with ground-pounding pre-Nader horsepower.

This muscle car collection is truly diverse in models and manufacturers; however, we have specialized in several categories: Hemi convertibles, big-block Camaros and big-block Corvettes.

In a sense, the Hemi convertible is an oxymoron from the standpoint that true muscle car enthusiasts would never have ordered a convertible in the sixties or early seventies. Convertibles were heavier, slower and more expensive, and therefore far too impractical for the performance purists. For these reasons, production was extremely low and today these convertible behemoths are highly treasured examples of muscle on wheels.

The Central Office Production Order (COPO) Camaro epitomizes the muscle pony car. Stuffed with a factory 427 steel-block engine and, in some rare instances, the aluminum 427 engine, this mighty mite was the terror of the street and strip. It was truly a race car in street clothing. And imagine, it was obtainable from the local dealer.

The Corvettes (along with the Cobras) present an enigma in a sense: they are considered not only muscle cars but also true sports cars. Corvette's L-72 steel-block, the L-88 aluminum-head engine and, of course, the legendary ZL-1 aluminum engines made Corvettes fierce quarter-mile competitors. These Corvettes were built for straight-line business and wore the muscle image on their big-block sleeves.

Prominent automobile collections take on their own personalities, and Vintage is no exception. Similar to living organisms, they change and grow and have even been known to die. Yet, throughout the evolution of this ongoing process, three variables are constants: the joy of the hunt, the pleasure of the acquisition and the challenge of the authentic restoration. This collection is not finished and will continue to evolve and grow for years to come.

The Vintage muscle car collection was conceived with great thought and care. However, this achievement would never have been possible without the patronage and enthusiasm of Otis Chandler. Through his foresight, Otis has changed the direction of automobile collecting for many generations to come.

Greg Joseph
Curator
Vintage Museum of Transportation and Wildlife

The cars of the Vintage collection
Muscle cars
1963 Shelby American AC Cobra 289
1964 Dodge Ramcharger Superstock
1967 Chevrolet Corvette L-71 Tri-Power
1967 Ford Fairlane 500 XL-R 427
1967 Plymouth GTX Hemi convertible
1967 Shelby American Cobra 427
1968 Chevrolet Corvette L-88 convertible
1968 Plymouth GTX Hemi convertible
1968½ Ford Mustang GT Super Cobrajet
1969 Chevrolet Camaro Baldwin Motion Phase III

1969 Chevrolet Camaro Yenko/SC, four-speed
1969 Chevrolet Camaro Yenko/SC, automatic
1969 Chevrolet Camaro COPO
1969 Chevrolet Camaro ZL-1
1969 Chevrolet Camaro Z-28, four-wheel disc brakes
1969 Chevrolet Chevelle Yenko/SC
1969 Chevrolet Corvette Baldwin Motion Phase III
1969 Chevrolet Corvette L-88 convertible
1969 Chevrolet Corvette ZL-1 coupe
1969 Chevrolet Nova Yenko
1969 Dodge Charger Daytona Hemi
1969 Dodge Coronet R/T Hemi convertible
1969 Ford Mustang Mach I Super Cobrajet
1969 Ford Torino Super Cobrajet coupe
1970 Buick Gran Sport GSX Stage I
1970 Chevrolet Chevelle SS Baldwin Motion Phase III 454
1970 Dodge Challenger R/T Hemi convertible
1970 Dodge Challenger R/T Hemi coupe
1970 Dodge Challenger T/A 340 Six-Pack
1970 Dodge Charger R/T SE
1970 Dodge Coronet R/T Hemi convertible
1970 Oldsmobile 4-4-2 W-30 convertible
1970 Oldsmobile 4-4-2 W-30 coupe
1970 Plymouth 'Cuda AAR 340 Six-Pack coupe
1970 Plymouth 'Cuda Hemi convertible
1970 Plymouth 'Cuda Hemi coupe
1970 Pontiac GTO Judge convertible
1971 Chevrolet Corvette ZR-1 LT-1 coupe
1971 Chevrolet Corvette ZR-2 454 convertible
1971 Dodge Challenger R/T Hemi coupe
1971 Dodge Charger R/T 440 Six-Pack coupe
1971 Dodge Charger R/T Hemi coupe
1971 Dodge Charger Super Bee 440 Six-Pack coupe
1971 Dodge Charger Super Bee Hemi coupe
1971 Plymouth 'Cuda convertible
1971 Plymouth 'Cuda coupe

1971 Plymouth Road Runner Hemi coupe
1972 Chevrolet Chevelle SS 454
1974 Dodge Dart Sport Hang 10 coupe

Classic, race and sports cars
1958 Porsche 356 Speedster
1965 Porsche 356C coupe
1965 Porsche SC coupe
1965 Porsche 356 cabriolet
1969 Porsche 917K
1973 Porsche 911S
1979 Porsche 935 twin-turbo
1982 Porsche 930S turbo
1989 Porsche 911 Speedster
1989 Porsche 959
1982 Toyota Celica race car coupe
1985 Ferrari 288 GTO
1988 Chevrolet Callaway twin-turbo convertible
1989 Chevrolet Corvette ZR-1 prototype convertible
1989 Lamborghini Countach 25th Anniversary
1989 Pontiac Trans Am 25th Anniversary coupe
1990 Ferrari Testarossa
1990 Ferrari F40

Miscellaneous
1894 Baldwin Steam locomotive
1911 Mack chain-drive stake-bed truck
1917 American LaFrance fire engine
1923 Ahrens-Fox fire engine
1929 Ford Model A fire chief's pickup truck
1931 Duesenberg Derham four-door Tourster
1933 Packard 12 Dietrich Car of the Dome
1933 Isotta-Fraschini Tipo 8A-SS Castagna dual-cowl phaeton
1934 Packard 12 LeBaron boat-tail speedster
1937 Pierce Arrow Travelodge Model A travel trailer
1939 Ford Deluxe Woody station wagon
1940 Indian motorcycle

Rise and Fall of the American Muscle Car

It was such an ambitious project that it's a wonder Congress didn't recoil into a filibuster at the proposed cost. Yet the automobile was everybody's darling and auto makers were speeding the national recovery from a world war and a police action. And when Dwight Eisenhower proposed a full-fledged nation-wide interstate highway system, it provoked smiles of wonder and admiration for the grandness of the scheme.

If goods that moved by train still had to be transported by truck at either end, why not

The Hemi, previous page, 1964 Dodge Ramcharger Superstock two-door hardtop: 426 ci, 425 hp from dual four-barrel carburetors. Above, the hood-mounted tachometer from the 1970 Pontiac GTO Judge Ram Air IV convertible: 400 ci, 355 hp.

transport them by truck in the middle too? If goods, then why not people? After all, American Motors called its great new car a Rambler. Didn't that suggest something?

So it was budgeted. Only wars had cost more. The Pentagon, covetous of federal monies when available, argued in behalf of this one, suggesting that a far-reaching system such as this would aid in the defensive movement of troops, should the unthinkable ever become reality. Thus, 41,000 miles of high-speed, limited-access free highways were to be built. The system would serve town and country. It would link supplier to manufacturer to distributor to customer. It would doom mass transit in the United States.

The glorious twenties and thirties, the glamorous days of automobiling, were being

brought back. And the US government was going to pay 90 cents on the dollar at nearly $1 million per mile. It was 1956. *Time* magazine honored General Motors president Harlow Curtice as Man of the Year. There were write-in votes in presidential primaries for the Rambler's father, George Romney.

Chrysler Corporation began the muscle car era five years earlier when it introduced its first V–8. The hemispherical-head engine unleashed a performance war that brought the American car buyer right through the Golden Age of automobiles. But the Golden Age went unrecognized until years later; like most great moments, it was appreciated only after we blinked and it was gone.

In 1956, General Motors had named Semon E. "Bunkie" Knudsen as general man-

Rear wheel and exhaust pipe from the 1969 Chevrolet Camaro Baldwin Motion Phase III: 427 ci, 500 hp.

It was the Golden Age of the automobile, and there were write-in votes in presidential primaries for the Rambler's father, George Romney

ager of Pontiac Division. Knudsen hired Elliott M. "Pete" Estes to be chief engineer. Estes in turn plucked thirty-three-year-old John Zachary DeLorean from Packard and created an Advanced Engineering Department for him.

Before 1958, the Automobile Manufacturers Association (AMA) banned its members from participating in racing. This ban was honored by some members, ignored by others and flaunted openly by the rest. An era had begun.

In May 1959, Ford Motor Company won a trademark battle against Chrysler over use of the name Falcon, and Rodger Ward won the Indy 500 in a Leader Card Special, at 138.6 mph.

A month later, Carroll Shelby codrove an Aston Martin to win the 24 Hours of Le Mans in France. Roger Smith and Efrem Zimbalist, Jr., asked Edd Byrnes to park their car at 77 Sunset Strip and lend them his comb.

In October, Chrysler Corporation removed the Hemi engine from regular production, introducing its B series, the 413 ci engines. The West German government returned ownership of the Volkswagen factories to private hands. By the end of November, the Edsel was history. In the same year, Americans read Ian Fleming's *Goldfinger* and learned of some options not regularly available on an Aston Martin—a COPO Aston?

At the end of the fifties, Dwight Eisenhower was President of the United States. A year later, the country had not only changed presidents, nor merely ended a decade; it had changed generations. It had gone from wearing a homburg on its head and a scarf around its neck to displaying the hatless, coatless, brusque brashness of youth.

Bunkie Knudsen knew it. Pete Estes and John DeLorean knew it. Lee Iacocca certainly

knew it. But so did Zora Arkus-Duntov, Bill Mitchell, Gene Bordinat, Bob McCurry, Lynn Townsend and David E. Davis.

In 1960, an American exodus had reached lemming proportions. Suburbs offered peace, quiet, space. The interstate highway system had made automobiles a key element in a new American way of life. Washington announced that the 1959 gross national product was $400 billion. The economy, if not soaring, was motoring away.

Bill Mitchell, chief of styling for General Motors, took his daughter's birthday present and, at the direction of advertising executive David E. Davis, displayed it at the Chicago Auto Show. The Corvair Monza showed buyers and car builders alike that compact did not always mean boring.

In April, the California legislature in Sacramento approved the United States' first smog control bill. The next month, Jim Rathman won the Indy 500 but 100 spectators were hurt from the collapse of their viewing scaffolds.

In September, four Mideast countries, Iran, Iraq, Kuwait and Saudi Arabia, took responsibility for their own future and formed the Organization of Petroleum Exporting Countries (OPEC).

By year-end, John F. Kennedy had won the US presidency by fewer than 115,000 votes. Kennedy had campaigned successfully using a strategy of constructive criticism. While Nixon Republicans boasted of nearly fifty percent increases in personal income and gross national product, Kennedy suggested to Americans they could do better. And when all the votes were in, the narrowest margin of victory in recent election history inducted the energy of youth into the Capitol. Kennedy was born in the twentieth century, and that made him one of us. His entire life had occurred since the automobile.

In February 1961, Marvin Panch averaged 149.6 mph to win Daytona in one of Smokey Yunick's cast-off Pontiacs. What AMA ban?

During the fall of 1961, Carroll Shelby learned that AC Cars might fold, Lynn Townsend was named president of Chrysler and Pontiac introduced the Tempest. In addition, Lee Iacocca was shown a new car based on a Falcon chassis. Iacocca knew Henry Ford II had to see it and he knew America had to have it.

Zora Arkus-Duntov was given the go-ahead to begin a race car project using a new Sting Ray in early 1962, and before the summer was over, Carroll Shelby had moved to Venice, California, and begun building his dream. Roy Lunn and a band of engineers produced a two-seat Mustang prototype in just 100 days. Before the end of 1962, Bunkie Knudsen was promoted out of Pontiac and into Chevrolet.

In a January 1963 paper to the Society of Automotive Engineers, Roy Lunn and his engineers warned all readers of the coming Golden Age: "Sports cars are by their nature controversial: they arouse the interest of the adolescent—and of those reaching second childhood; they excite the otherwise calm—and accentuate the egotistical; they are admired by many—and purchased by comparatively few." (Reprinted by permission. SAE paper 611F, Roy Lunn, January 14-18, 1963.) Also in January 1963, General Motors reported a $1.4 billion profit for 1962, a record. Within the next months, Ford Motor Company negotiated with Ferrari to purchase the Italian car maker. But too many lawyers negotiated too much and Enzo Ferrari withdrew his offer to sell.

April 1963 saw Lynn Townsend mandate victory at Daytona. Ford introduced an air-conditioned Thunderbird, and the Corvette Grand Sport first appeared in an SCCA race in Maryland. Hertz was dropping Americans out of the sky and putting them in the driver's seat.

During the long summer of 1963, Craig Breedlove zipped across the Bonneville Salt Flats at 407 mph. Through the fall, Chevrolet launched the Sting Ray with Bill Mitchell's stylish split rear windows, and sold more than 10,500 coupes but nearly 11,000 convertibles. The US population topped 189 million, the average age of Americans was 29½, the combined income in four of ten American families was $7,000 and the United States counted close to 100,000 millionaires. Freddie Lorenzen won six NASCAR Grand Nationals in 1963 and grossed more than $113,000 in prize money, edging out Arnold Palmer by more than $10,000.

In early 1964, Carroll Shelby shoehorned a 427 ci NASCAR engine into his Cobra and Richard Petty introduced 426 ci Hemi power to American racing fans, leading three other Mopar Hemis to sweep clean the Daytona 500 and proclaiming the Golden Age open. Ford wedged its 427 into a Fairlane, producing a mighty dragster, but since the performance parameters included turning at very high speed, it went back to the drawing board. The introduction of Ford's Mustang coincided with the opening of the New York World's Fair.

In May, Plymouth presented its Barracuda, with the largest back window glass in production. A. J. Foyt proved his worth by winning at Indianapolis.

By summer's end, the first privately owned Hemi-engined automobile had slipped out of Dodge and was living and racing out of St. Johns, Michigan. By year-end, Art Arfons

Hone-A-Drive mechanical overdrive from the 1970 Chevrolet Chevelle Baldwin Motion Phase III: 454 ci, 500 hp.

Dual Holley carburetors and air cleaner from the 1967 Ford Fairlane 500 XL-R coupe: 427 ci, 425 hp.

"Sports cars are by their nature controversial: they arouse the interest of the adolescent—and of those reaching second childhood; they excite the otherwise calm—and accentuate the egotistical"

ran 536.7 mph at Bonneville, and 32,000 Pontiac GTOs and 303,000 Mustangs were sold.

In January 1965, the Government Services Administration published its seventeen automobile safety standards. Comment was invited.

On May 30, Jimmy Clark won the Indianapolis 500, driving a Lotus and averaging 150.7 mph.

On July 13, at Senate Subcommittee Hearings on Executive Reorganization, Senator Abraham Ribicoff called to the hearing room General Motors chairman Frederic Donner, president James Roche and chief engineer Harry Barr. Ribicoff had many questions regarding the safety of General Motors products.

After steady questioning, it became apparent that the General Motors senior officers were not sufficiently prepared for the detail demanded. In an effort to expand on a previous answer, chairman Donner announced that GM had only the week before arranged a four-year, $250,000 per year grant to Massachusetts Institute of Technology for research into "all aspects of the safety problem." It was known that Donner's annual salary was three times larger.

It got worse. Sitting on Ribicoff's committee was Senator Robert F. Kennedy. Annoyed by what seemed inadequate research into vehicle safety, Kennedy pressed. He asked what General Motors' profit had been in 1964. Donner hesitated (it had been a record, published in newspapers), then answered that it was $1.7 billion. Kennedy repeated the figure and then confirmed that of that sum, $1 million was to be spent on safety? Donner clarified: "In this particular facet." Kennedy quickly did math: "If you just gave one percent of your profits, that would be $17 million."

Before it had even really gotten started, the era of the muscle car was seriously jeopardized. Another attorney on the Ribicoff committee sat listening. As a junior lawyer, he was learning. His name was Ralph Nader.

Later in July, John DeLorean was promoted to general manager, Pontiac Division. In the fall, Dodge introduced the Coronet just as the 426-S (street) Hemi was in final development.

By the end of 1965, Carroll Shelby's Cobra won the World Championship, Pontiac split the GTO off into a line of its own and Don Yenko had founded Yenko Sports Cars at his Canonsburg, Pennsylvania, dealership. In 1965, Americans were shocked and enraged by Ralph Nader's book *Unsafe at Any Speed*.

In February 1966, Richard Petty fulfilled Bob McCurry's mandate and won Daytona. In March, GM president James Roche publicly apologized to Ralph Nader for the smear investigation the auto maker had conducted on the attorney. Fifty investigators, working under orders to "find something, get this guy," found nothing. By April, General Motors recalled 1.5 million cars. Henry Ford warned Congress not "to do anything irrational" about car safety, that critics such as Ralph Nader "really don't know anything about safety." Later that month, Ford recalled 30,000 cars for brake problems. And concluding the auto industry's longest month of 1966, the US Supreme Court ruled that General Motors had violated antitrust laws.

Graham Hill won the 1966 Indianapolis 500, averaging 144.3 mph. Over the summer, Ford-powered cars drove 3,009 miles through the French countryside, averaged 125.4 mph for twenty-four hours, crossed the finish line first and won Le Mans. In September, Lyndon B. Johnson named William Haddon first director of the National Transportation Safety Agency and signed the automobile safety law.

It seemed that though Americans got wealthier, the times stayed the same. Little happened in 1967 that they could brag about even a year later. Millions of automobiles were recalled by their makers and the United Auto Workers struck Ford Motor Company for forty-six days. The US census reached 200 million, and LBJ signed the air quality act and budgeted $428 million (slightly more than $10,000 per interstate mile) to fight air pollution.

On February 6, 1968, Bunkie Knudsen drove across town and started his new job as president of Ford Motor Company. Bobby Unser won Indy at 152.9 mph in the Rislone Special. By the end of 1968, three of four Ford designers were younger than thirty-five; the average age was the mid-twenties at GM and only twenty-seven at Chrysler.

In January 1969, John DeLorean was promoted to general manager of Chevrolet. In the first quarter of the year, General Motors recalled 6 million automobiles for inspections and repairs.

In February 1969, General Motors announced that it had begun developing engines to use the newly introduced unleaded gasoline. Insurance agents got their copies of *Reflector*, a trade journal featuring a special report on muscle cars and explaining "What's Behind the Surcharge." The journal identified muscle cars as midsize cars with at least 300 hp. Its data indicated that these cars would account for six percent of the total car market in 1970, yet Nationwide Mutual Insurance research showed the same cars produced fifty-six percent more losses than did more mundane cars. Calling the cars "over-powered," Nationwide planned a fifty percent surcharge;

State Farm planned a similar twenty-five percent increase. The cost of playing in the Golden Age was to rise rapidly.

On New Year's Eve, 1970, President Richard Nixon signed the law that aimed to reduce automobile pollution emissions ninety percent by 1977.

In early 1971, Abu Dhabi joined OPEC and together decided to set oil prices without consulting their customers in advance. Rolls-Royce declared bankruptcy, owing to the costs of producing new jet engines for the Lockheed Tri-Star airplane.

In March, the British government offered Rolls-Royce $144 million (£60 million) in aid. Ford recalled all its Pintos for engine problems. On May 19, Chrysler Corporation installed the last Hemi engine into the last convertible.

In October, the snowmobile world speed record was set at 140.2 mph. In the last days of the year, Washington removed the federal excise tax on automobiles.

In January of 1972, Chrysler offered no Hemis and no convertibles. Camaro offered nothing larger than a 396, and Corvette's LS-5 rated only 270 hp; nothing that weak had even been available since 1965. All the Bosses were fired from Mustang's line-up, and the heaviest hitter remaining was a 351 regular gas burner. On March 6, 1972, beginning its ninth year of production, the Mustang was named Car of the Decade by *Popular Hot Rodding* magazine.

In 1963, Roy Lunn had concluded his paper to the SAE with this statement: "The Mustang is a high-spirited animal with possibilities and limitations still to be established." In 1972, few possibilities remained. It was all over but the applause.

The 1970 Plymouth 'Cuda Hemi convertible: 426 ci, 425 hp. Cold air induction was standard equipment.

1964 Dodge Ramcharger Superstock 426 Hemi Cross Ram

For The Little Old Lady From Pasadena

Inside the glove compartment, found almost by accident, there's a small yellow sticker, about 1½ by 3 inches. In the past, it would have been hidden, blocked from view by winter gloves, road maps, Kleenex tissue packets, a tin of aspirin.

"Notice. This car is equipped with a 426 cu. in. engine (and other special equipment). This car is intended for use in supervised acceleration trials and is not for highway or for general passenger car use.

"Accordingly, the vehicle is sold 'AS IS' and the 12-month or 12,000 mile vehicle warranty coverage and 5–year or 50,000 mile power train warranty coverage does not apply to this vehicle."

Chrysler engineers remember that stick-

The Dodge Superstock was the car of choice of little old ladies from Pasadena in a song made famous by singers Jan and Dean. The car was limited in production to only 50: a dozen were factory race cars with steel bodies dipped in acid to dissolve away metal for lightness.

er. At one meeting, product planners, engineers and marketing people wondered about warranties. They decided they wouldn't honor warranties: they could only imagine how the cars would be used.

For this is one of the real Ramchargers. Fifty factory Superstock Dodge 440 two-door sedans were produced, but only a dozen were acid-dipped, factory optional lightweights. Just slam a door, and that hollow, thin tin clunk would have put off most buyers who regard a solid slam as part of a new car test.

Kick the tires. They're 7.50x14, skinny enough to keep lit up through second gear if the driver is of a mind to do so.

Back in January 1964, a twenty-three-year-old farm implement mechanic was of a mind to do just that. Lynn Ferguson collected his money, priced the competition, then gave his money to Lundy Motors, the local Dodge dealer in his hometown of St. Johns, Michigan.

"I raced a '51 Ford six-cylinder, off and on," says Ferguson, "a casual-type thing. But

This was probably the first 426 ci Hemi engined Chrysler product delivered to a non-professional racer; it was the only two-door hardtop Hemi known produced in 1964. A large hood air scoop differentiated it from any other 440 on the way to the grocery. Instruments were minimal and the interior was simple street stock. Dodge presumed that all the earliest 426 Hemis were going to bona fide racers who would gut the interiors and add the aftermarket instruments of their choice. The early 426 Hemis had chrome valve covers, opposite page. Decals were used, but not on the outside bodywork. The air cleaner warned drivers to close needle valves when switching fuels; inside the glovebox another decal told the owner there was no warranty on the car.

you're nowhere near 'fastest guy on the block' with a six . . . in fact you get laughed at. So when I ordered a new car, I figured since I had no romantic interest in my life, I could put all my money into a winner. I'd get something that wouldn't be laughed at."

Ferguson ordered the 426 ci Max Wedge Stage III 415 hp engine in a two-door hardtop, and he patiently endured four months of no news before he got the bad news: Wedge engines were out of production, and a new engine and transmission would be fitted. Because Ferguson liked the Dodge's looks better than its competition, he stuck it out. Another six weeks passed until dealer Red Lundy called to tell Ferguson that his Hemi, as a specialty vehicle, could be picked up at the Dodge factory, ninety miles away.

Around dusk, Ferguson and Lundy showed up. Three other Hemis were there for delivery too, each sporting a $620 option Ferguson could not afford (the aluminum front end) and each awaiting a transporter to take it home.

Ferguson had paid cash, $3,820.25, and Lundy had driven Ferguson to Detroit "to save the extra $13.50 shipping," says Ferguson. "But in the first block I couldn't get it from second to third, so I drove it back to the factory." A quick linkage adjustment rendered the trip no more remarkable than any other drive out of Detroit. Except, that is, for a 1500 rpm idle and solid lifters clattering like Michigan State's marching band.

That night, home in quiet St. Johns, Ferguson took a first long look at his life savings. He later recalled it as a Plain Jane easily mistaken for a six with a hood scoop. But as rare as hood scoops were in 1964, a passerby asked him why he'd ever put a hole in the hood of his brand-new car.

Sitting in the car now, the superstiff bench seat raises questions of how many other police car parts saw duty in street racers. A slightly elliptical steering wheel sticks out from a dashboard almost devoid of instrumentation. A massive white billiard ball sits atop the dog-legged Hurst shifter lever, surrounded by a sea of plush carpeting.

Ferguson's car has a heater, usually deleted by the factory to discourage street use of what were essentially race cars. Even with no radio, imagine Ferguson dating his future wife in this car, going to the drags. His wife would eventually drive it to the market.

Lumbering around a parking lot, the low gears whine loudly. But fight the stiff competition clutch down and lever the gas pedal forward, and the car comes alive. Putting the pedal to the floor produces modern performance art; the engine explodes, its sound bores into the ears. The tortured suspension swings and reacts.

The sound is up front but quickly it moves under you as you come out of the hole. The front end comes up, the back end goes down, all the slack and elasticity are wrenched out of the tires. The whole car levers back up and launches.

"After I'd been home a week I just had to hear what it sounded like with the caps off," says Ferguson. "I pulled it far away from the barn. My dad was milking the cows at the time. When I fired it up, they all kicked their milking machines off.

"My dad had been raised around machinery but he came out of the barn pretty upset. So we allowed as how we wouldn't do that again. But then he got curious to hear it himself, so we started it again. What we didn't know was Mom had gone back in and hooked up all the cows again. We started the car and

ALWAYS CLOSE NEEDLE VALVES
BEFORE SWITCHING FROM ONE
FUEL TO ANOTHER • WHEN BOTH
VALVES ARE OPEN AT ONE TIME
THE FUELS WILL MIX • THIS
MAKES IT IMPOSSIBLE TO START

all the cows kicked off the milking machines again!"

Ferguson campaigned the car in NHRA AA/Stock class during 1964, then in the newly created B/Modified Production class in 1965. His mid-twelve-second, 110+ mph runs fit his class, and he humiliated most all comers.

In early 1966, Ferguson married "the only girl I ever knew who didn't think gasoline clashed with perfume," and then he served military duty from May until October 1967. In 1980, he sold the car.

Marvin Hughes, in Ocala, Florida, was the last to own the car. For thirty years he has worked on Hemi engines, he says, "doing this so long it all seems common now. I worked on these race cars when they were brand new."

But Ferguson's car, he suggests, was uncommon. "As far as I know that is the only one ever produced like it. Probably it was the first

Cruising Colorado Boulevard, Pasadena, California. This was not the car for the low-and-slow cruising popular in the eighties. The Superstock Ramcharger 426 preferred to run— and any three-block stretch of Colorado equaled a quarter-mile.

one to go to some private guy. See, all the factory racers were two door sedans. This one was a hardtop. It's nothing but a pure old factory racer, and yet this guy ordered it. . . . I'm pretty sure it had to be the first one. Just because it's a hardtop."

From the start, Dodge used frames from convertibles for Hemis. The reinforced frames resisted body twist. That was the reason all factory racers were two-door sedans; the center post served as bracing.

First car, special car, uncommon car—it's all the same to Ferguson. "To this day, that car is still just a car," he says. "I didn't look at that car any different from if I had picked up a 427 Ford or Chevy. It was meant to be driven, to have fun with, to go park with, to go to the store with. The thing that amazed the kids was that it started up right now! Everyone expected something more temperamental because it was a race car.

"I have two sons." Ferguson gets quiet. "So maybe this was more. This car was my daughter; it really is like a daughter because the other guy got her, married her, you know, took her away. I guess all you do now is just keep in touch."

"This car is intended for use in supervised acceleration trials and is not for highway or for general passenger car use"

1967 Ford Fairlane 500 XL-R 427

Waging War With NASCAR

The 1964 Daytona 500 was a Mopar show. Richard Petty led two other Plymouth Hemis across the line without a Ford in sight. Ford, however, hung around the track the next day to test a new, smaller car. It had stuffed a 427 into the newly restyled Fairlane. But it didn't work. The nose-heavy lightweight handled poorly at big-oval speeds, and the idea was put on hold.

In 1963, Ford won twenty-three of fifty-five starts on NASCAR ovals. It took the championship and more than half the prize money paid in Grand National events. For

Aerodynamic in 1967 meant all the vertical surfaces were angled as though bent by the wind. When the best gas was less than 30 cents a gallon, the wind turbulence created by deeply spoked wheels and recessed window glass didn't matter. Ford's Top Loader four-speed was so named because the gears were installed through the top of the transmission casing. It took the strongest transmission Ford offered to handle 480 lb-ft of torque in this 3,350 lb coupe.

1964, one enthusiast magazine wondered in print if Galaxies would win them all. They won only thirty of sixty-two events, but took the championship again. The real rout came in 1965: Ford took forty-eight of fifty-five events.

The joy in Dearborn, Michigan, was virtually limitless. But across Detroit in Hamtramck, Michigan, Chrysler was taking notes. By 1963, it was working on a 426 ci version of the Hemi. It was ready for Daytona in the dawn of 1964. As speeds rose above 170 mph, a flurry of questions rose as well.

The NASCAR rules required that 1,500 examples be scheduled or produced during the competition year for an engine to be race legal. No one had ever seen a Hemi Dodge or Plymouth in a showroom (Chrysler sold only 493 in 1964—to drag racers). Yet NASCAR was doing what it had often done best: circumventing its own rules to encourage manufacturers.

If NASCAR's big ovals were battlegrounds, outright war was declared almost

immediately. Ford asked NASCAR chief Bill France for permission to run its new engine, a 427 ci with a single overhead cam. Permission was denied, but Ford opened Pandora's box; none of the other competitors had a clue it existed—and in fact, it didn't! Barely finished by February, the engine wasn't yet even in a car.

The 1965 NASCAR season was another Ford success, though to stay competitive with Chrysler, Ford decided to offer its 427 sohc for public sale. The only problem was the engine's $1,963 price, compared with $900 for the Hemi. France had little to say, but his new rules did the talking. "Legal" 119 inch wheelbase cars (the new Fairlane) were required to weigh 4,400 pounds, compared with 4,000 pounds for the Hemis. Ford, in the person of Henry II, withdrew from NASCAR for the first part of the 1966 season.

When NASCAR rules for 1967 were published, they allowed the sohc engine and Ford was ready to go back. The engine was not used, though. Ralph Nader's 1966 book *Unsafe at Any Speed* had made everyone safety conscious. Ford feared that offering a 600+ hp engine to the public might seem irresponsible and might bring unwanted attention from Washington.

So the car was to be the yet-again-redesigned Fairlane fastback, but with the exist-

A car complete in every detail, the engine starting instructions were still wrapped around the driver's sun visor. And Indian Head Ethyl super-premium gasoline was still 27 cents at the pumps. The Rock Store, near Malibu, California, opposite, is a well-known destination for mountain road bikers and road racers. Otis Chandler, right, chats with fellow cyclist Patrick Downs. Manhandling the long-wheelbase XL-R around canyon roads is out of character for a car groomed for super ovals and quarter-mile straights.

ing 427 race engine. The complicated rules of NASCAR now even allowed some creative solutions to aerodynamic and roadholding problems. So in August 1966, the first race to use 1967 rules, Ford returned.

The weight formula suggested that a sleeved, 396 ci version of the 427 be tried, as the car could weigh 3,700 pounds and this lighter weight might save fuel and brake and tire wear. It did, and Freddie Lorenzen ran away with the next race. But it was too late in the season, and despite winning four of the last five races, Ford finished third behind Dodge and Plymouth in 1966. It came back and placed second to Plymouth in 1967.

With its vinyl roof, the street version of the NASCAR racer looks like a six-cylinder to-market, to-market coupe, lacking only whitewall tires and imitation wire wheel covers. Even the interior is misleading, with no instruments but a speedometer and gas gauge. An otherwise sixties high-tech chrome and black interior is interrupted by what may have been a product planner's victory over a design engineer: an imitation wood steering wheel.

The R engine peaked at 425 hp at 6000 rpm with two Holley 4V carburetors. The W, lesser by a small degree, produced 420 hp at 5600 rpm with a single Holley. At idle, the XL-R even sounds like a race engine. But engine

A rare sight, previous page: the R engine with 427 ci, 425 hp, dual four-barrel carburetors. Less than 60 of these cars were built in 1967. This street package legalized Ford's challenge against Chrysler Hemi supremacy on the super ovals. The perfect grocery shopper's coupe as the deep trunk could easily fit food for a growing family—or an entire NASCAR crew. It's also easy to imagine a 55 gallon drum of moonshine whiskey nestled inside.

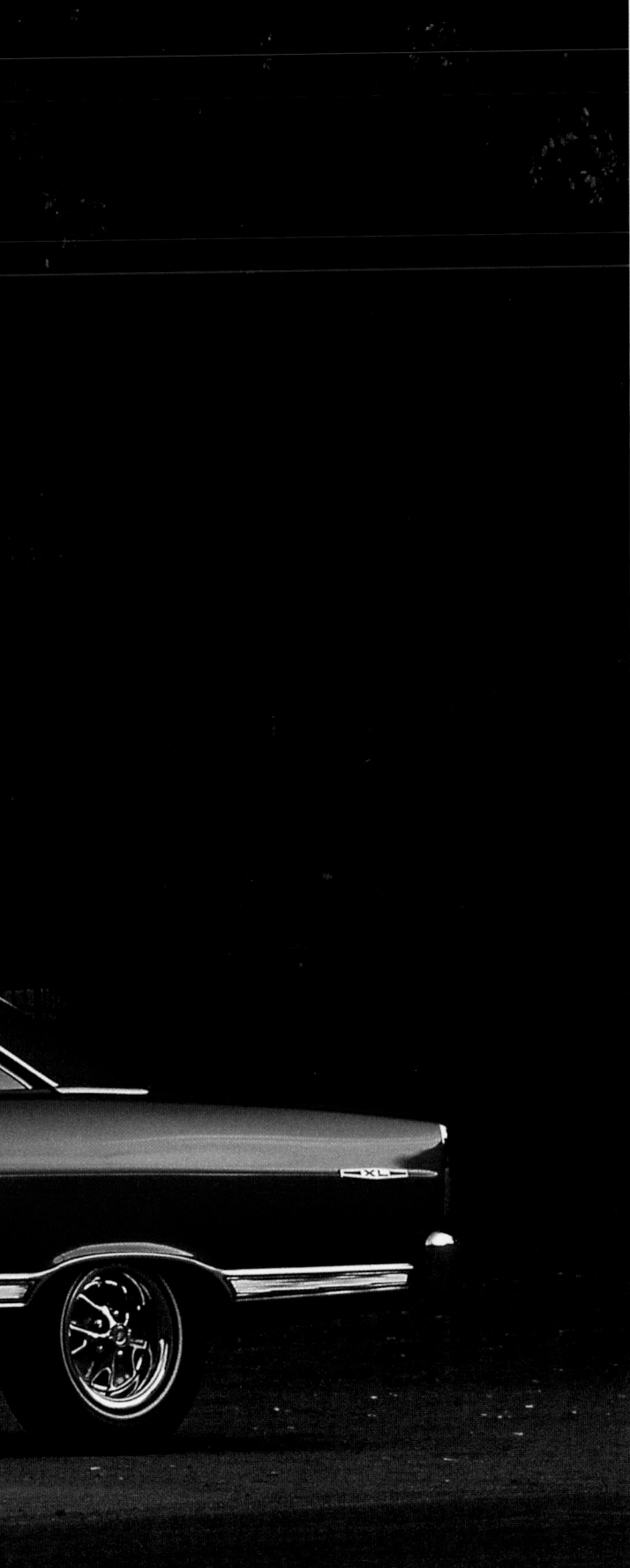

noise is baffled at speed and all goes out the tailpipe. Slow down and the sound comes back to the car, rather as the stern waves come back and lift a speedboat after the throttles are cut.

Handling this car at any kind of speed is hard work on the street. Its long wheelbase (119 inches; 11 inches longer than the Mustang's), ultrastiff competition clutch and unassisted steering are not for the power-assisted generation. With the proper modifications, though, it's possible to imagine this car racing the high Daytona banks, Mario Andretti at the wheel, on the way to victory.

Warm lights, cold drinks and a phone are the keys to the success of the Rock Store. Fastback styling, long wheelbase and 427 engine were the keys to the Fairlane's success on the NASCAR ovals.

The street version of the NASCAR racer looked like a six-cylinder to-market, to-market coupe, lacking only whitewall tires and imitation wire wheel covers

1967 Shelby American Cobra 427

American Muscle Meets Classic British Sports Car

If his plans had worked out, the badges on Carroll Shelby's Cobras would have read Powered by Chevrolet. Even in the mid-fifties, Shelby recognized that there must be a life after racing, but he knew that racing could start that life. His life was to build a car with plenty of power, yet that would be economical to purchase, operate and maintain. He envisioned an American V-8 in a European body.

His friends envisioned bankruptcy or the nut house. They shook their heads and reminded him of Sydney Herbert Allard, a Briton. Allard dropped big American V-8s—Cadillacs, flathead Fords, Chryslers and Lincolns—into his own cars. He won races and eventually sold some road cars. Another person, American Briggs Swift Cunningham, had loads of meat-packing money and produced his own cars in his own factory, putting more American V-8s—more Cadillacs and Chryslers—into more cars. And what came out of Cunningham's West Palm Beach, Florida, address were big, heavy, loss leaders. Cunningham, with all

While Carroll Shelby's Cobras battled around the world, American GIs did battle around Southeast Asia. Phantoms and Crusaders went out to wage war. Shelby's Cobras went out like the reserves, as weekend warriors. Twenty years later the survivors tell the tales. The 427 Cobra seating position shot the driver's feet off toward the front tire. Instrument panels differed greatly between street and full competition versions; a large tach sat directly in front of the driver for racers and semi-racers. A speedometer shared the space on street cars.

his wealth, gave up his cars before his money gave out.

Wisely, Shelby never even mentioned to his friends his real concern: current racing rules required a 183 ci engine, and no one in the United States built one.

Therefore, Shelby drove other people's Ferraris and chose his confidants more carefully. Two he trusted were Ed Cole, then a General Motors vice president and Chevrolet's general manager, and Harley Earl, Cole's chief engineer. Through 1956 and 1957, Shelby talked and they listened. But less visionary powers prevailed. Chevrolet's own Corvette was without identity (these were early years of Zora Arkus-Duntov) and sales were poor. Taking on another two-seat project met objections, and finally Cole passed on Shelby's ideas.

So Shelby continued racing, in 1958 and 1959 for Aston Martin, and continued dreaming of a 300 hp Austin-Healey. Racing in Europe would give him better opportunities to

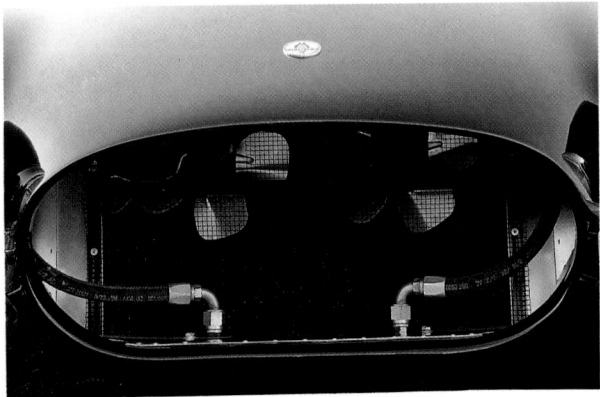

learn how to build his dream. The Europeans heard American gas-guzzling V-8s in their marketplace, the Americans heard two-seaters in theirs—and nobody liked what they heard. And Shelby began hearing laughter.

Then in June 1959, Carroll Shelby and Roy Salvadori won the 24 Hours of Le Mans for Aston Martin. For Shelby, it brought a new level of legitimacy.

Success brought opportunities. Representing Goodyear at Pikes Peak on July 4, 1961, he met Dave Evans, Ford's stock car racing boss. In September, Shelby learned that AC Cars of Surrey, England, might close since its engine supplier stopped making car engines. Shelby knew AC cars and wasted no time, proposing to the company that it mate a V-8 (he didn't even know whose yet) with its chassis. Days later, Shelby, who still leaned toward GM, learned that Ford had perfected casting processes yielding lighter-weight engines at lower cost. Then AC's owner, Charles Hurlock, answered, encouraging Shelby, who immediately wrote to Evans in Dearborn.

Corvettes had begun racing in early 1956, with Zora Arkus-Duntov's assistance. By 1961, Corvettes meant racing and performance; the Thunderbird had become a four-seat, four-

Shelby's competition 427 Cobra used one 780 cfm Holley four-barrel atop Ford's 427 side-oiler cast-iron race engine. Producing 490 hp, it would accelerate the 2,150 lb racer from 0–100–0 mph in under 14 sec., something difficult even for an F-4 Phantom. Cooling fans came standard on the street big-block Cobras, as well as the S/C semi-competition cars. This Cobra began life as a street version. In 1977 it was rebuilt to full competition specs but the fans were kept. Naugahyde bucket seats were standard in the competition and S/C versions, opposite. Road cars got leather. The engine, set far back in the chassis for weight distribution, needed a reverse bend in the gearshift.

door boulevardier. Dave Evans didn't wait for the mail. He called Shelby to offer him two new 221 ci V-8 engines.

The marriage was made in heaven. Evans soon called Shelby's shop in suburban Los Angeles, to offer two more engines, 260 ci versions. Shelby scraped together airfare and flew to England to supervise the birth of his dream. In February 1962, CSX0001 (Carroll Shelby Experimental number one) immigrated to the United States, christened after another of Shelby's dreams, the Cobra.

Now Shelby called Evans. He had to convince Ford to advance him enough engines to get the car going; if he could do that, he could convince Hurlock to produce enough cars for the engines. Evans saw the car, breathed carefully and introduced Shelby to Don Frey, head of engineering planning for Ford.

Frey, the Cobra's new father-in-law, had driven an Allard in the early fifties and knew exactly what Shelby was after. Frey liked what he saw, and engines were offered on credit. Hurlock matched good faith for good faith, and Carroll Shelby's house of cards had a car in the driveway.

The Cobra cut its teeth competing against Chevrolet's new Sting Ray. The Cobra failed. The second Cobra built went back to Dearborn, and Ford engineers worked with Shelby's newly hired chief engineer Phil Remington. Together they sorted out problems and continued entering races, and along about mid 1962 a paying customer took delivery of the first "production" Cobra.

Capitalized with $40,000 from friends and his own savings, Shelby moved seventy-four more out the door in 1962; one in ten was a race car. The ambitious racing schedule spread the Cobra name worldwide and hinted to European teams that they'd best take note.

Ford knew that winning took time. Outside Shelby, it had followed its own agenda. By February 1963, it had negotiated to buy Ferrari, and the Italian's price dropped from $18 million to $10 million.

Ford's goal in acquiring Ferrari was to win Le Mans, and it stipulated that Ferrari-Ford, the new racing division born of the acquisition, withdraw from Formula One to concentrate on the GT race. Enzo Ferrari, long a supporter of Formula One, resented this condition, which he viewed as the beginning of his emasculation. He countered that Ford must withdraw from Carroll Shelby. Negotiations ended shortly after, and Ford watched carefully when Shelby and his Cobras went to Le Mans, in an effort managed by no less than Stirling Moss.

Ferrari dominated Le Mans in 1963, taking first through sixth. The best Cobra came seventh. Ford was encouraged. Shelby decided to enter all the European races for 1964, with a new aerodynamic coupe nearly 20 mph faster. The season yielded few outright wins but only a few failures; Ford's gamble on Carroll Shelby's dream nearly brought a World Championship.

The parallel agendas introduced the GT40s at Le Mans. Against twelve starting Ferraris, the GT40s retired and a Cobra finished fourth.

Chevrolet was stuffing new 396s into 1965 Corvettes for domestic racing and Ferrari wanted to legalize its new midengine cars for Europe. The merger of Ford's and Shelby's motivations required a new offspring. The big NASCAR 427 engine was the only solution, and one even ran Daytona in 1964 as a test. But installing it was not easy. It was a new car in almost every way, its chassis designed on a computer, another first. When completed, the

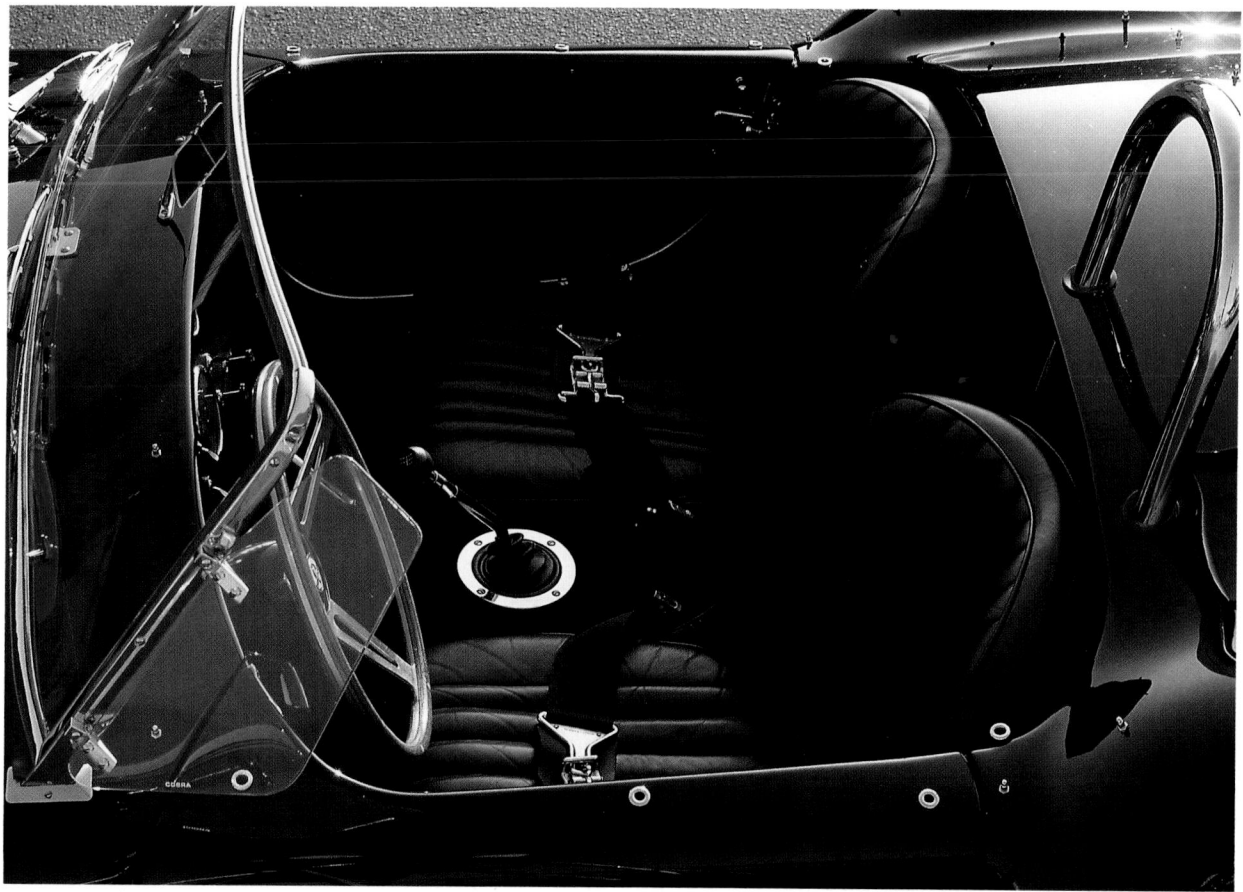

Cobra 427 CSX3001 resembled a 289 on steroids.

In the United States, the new car, designed to humble Corvette's new Grand Sport, was almost unbeatable. It won championships for three years straight. But the primary targets were Ferrari and the 1965 World Championship. Shelby planned a 427 coupe for that task.

International rules required that 100 race cars be built, but neither Ferrari nor Shelby had enough so both had to run their 1964 cars again in 1965. Ferrari protested and withdrew, leaving racing to private owners. Midyear, rules changed again, and only fifty of each model were needed for 1966. Once again,

Shelby found himself in the potential squeeze that had backed Ed Cole away.

Shelby's 427 Cobra now fit into the same class as Ford's GT40; each would compete against the other and against Ferrari. Shelby had built one 427 coupe and chassis for twenty-five more, but the project was killed.

Le Mans was a disaster in 1965. Eleven Fords in all varieties started, yet only one Cobra coupe finished, eighth. Nevertheless, Cobra, and Ford, won the World Championship based on performance everywhere else.

By the end of November 1965, Shelby had sold sixteen racing Cobras but still had thirty-four. Charles Beidler, the East Coast sales rep, suggested they be changed slightly and advertised as semi-competition (S/C) models, the fastest production cars ever offered.

The $9,500 race cars sold, but by then Shelby had been plucked from further Cobra development and put to work sorting out Ford's disappointing midengine GTs. There was to be no repeat of Le Mans 1965.

Throughout 1966, street Cobras used 428 police interceptor engines, which allowed owners a bit more drivability and Shelby a bit more profit. On roads and tracks, Shelby's Mustangs furthered his American legacy. But his personal efforts with the GTs paid off, delivering to himself and Ford their dream

Warriors. US Navy F–4 Phantom: 50,000 lb. Twin GE J79–15 engines. At 10,200 rpm, 34,000 lb thrust. Acceleration: 0–60 knots in some 6 sec., non-carrier takeoff. Off a carrier deck: 0–180 knots in 2.5 sec. USN Lt. Stan Jacobsen, Pacific Missile Test Center, Flight Weapons Section, knows about acceleration. Competition Cobras, opposite, used high-riser manifolds, 12.4:1 compression aluminum heads and tuned steel-tube headers, which burst out unmuffled just behind the front wheels. A 42 gallon gas tank filled most of the trunk.

come true, a Le Mans victory in 1966. With Henry Ford II himself looking on, Ford GTs crossed the finish line one-two-three, setting distance and speed records in the bargain.

Shelby's 1967 responsibilities centered around winning the World Championship for GT cars, and the 427 Cobras raced in the United States with privateers. His own Mustangs, winning US championships, sparked enthusiastic street sales.

As the GTs pulled him away from his Cobras, Shelby pondered the possibilities. He understood that fans lose interest in racing when the result is a foregone conclusion. When every series and championship is taken, when nothing remains to be won, could he justify the high cost of continuing to race? A firm believer that race wins Sunday sell cars Monday, Shelby wondered if too many race wins might even help the underdog. He concluded that there is a point at which it is best to withdraw for a while, to compete in other series or even not race.

In late December 1968, the last 427 Cobra was sold. Federal standards were to begin with the New Year. Exhaust emissions and safety almost seemed contradictions with regard to a 427 Cobra; the modifications would have diminished the mystique considerably. More to the point, the Cobras had won every championship, every series, had performed well in nearly every race.

The end was disappointing, Shelby would later remark, but he wasn't sure it was the wrong thing to do. Perhaps before anyone had a chance to lose interest, Shelby canceled his own dream.

In the end, the Cobras had won every championship, every series, and had performed well in nearly every race

1967 Plymouth GTX
426 Hemi convertible
1968 Plymouth GTX
426 Hemi convertible

Air Conditioning Not Available

Throughout most of the 1966 United States Auto Club eighteen-race season, each time Norm Nelson left the pits, he was driving a car most fans had never heard of before. When he won seven of the races and took the championship and Plymouth finally introduced the first production GTX, then the fans understood those three letters on the side of his bright, fast car.

For 1967, the top of the Belvedere line was a new performance car, designed as a muscle car, marketed as a muscle car. Offered as either a hardtop or a convertible, its styling took over where its engineering left off. Non-functional hood scoops mingled with an over-sized racing-style gas filler cap. The functional dual exhausts were tipped with chrome. Standard power was a 440 Super Commando,

In its first year of production, Plymouth sold only 17 GTX Hemi convertibles. This was an executive hot rod, purchased by someone who wanted the highest performance available in an open car, one of America's first muscle cars.

mated with a beefed-up TorqueFlite automatic transmission. A Special Performance Package offered a four-speed transmission and limited-slip rear end, and could be coupled with the already legendary 426 Hemi. After nearly three years of competition successes, the engine was finally offered for the street (of course, NASCAR cinched its availability in order to continue Plymouth's success in production-based lasses).

An even wilder version, called A/Stock, eliminated most of the sound insulation and moved the battery to the trunk to even weight distribution. The Hemi was standard. Lighter in weight and price than the GTXs, these were intended much more for the strip than for the street.

Street Hemis were not too severely detuned from racing engines. What's more, while NASCAR and USAC regulations limited the racers to a single four-barrel carburetor, the street cars could run duals. The engine still used solid-lifter camshafts, compression was

reduced to 10.25:1 and horsepower was still adequate at 425.

In organized, legal competition, GTXs won twenty-seven NASCAR races and the season championship with Richard Petty, the NHRA Springnationals with Sox and Martin, and the NHRA Winternationals with Don Grotheer. And then Plymouth restyled the car—top to bottom.

Surfaces once concave were now convex. Formerly flat planes became complex curves. Overall, the design became simpler, cleaner.

Again, muscular performance was a given. The standard engine was the 440. And in 1968, you could choose the four-speed over the TorqueFlite at no extra cost. The Hemi, again an option, was accompanied by serious chassis modifications as well: hardtops used the convertible frame, convertibles had extra torque boxes to tie the sides and rear end together. Even the frame members used to mount the engine were enlarged.

The 1968 Hemi GTX was not every man's street rod. The price started at around $3,300 for the hardtop. The Hemi packed another $605 (it had been $905 in 1967), while the mandatory automatic or four-speed transmission added nearly $200. Unlike the first

The front and rear vinyl seats were embossed to resemble hand-tooled leather. The rear bench seat was padded to simulate buckets. The console housed the TorqueFlite shifter and a second glovebox. Beneath the hood lived and breathed the resurrected Hemi. Throughout 1966, USAC racing fans saw Norm Nelson race a GTX but couldn't buy one themselves. Introduced to the public in 1967, Chrysler's muscle development program was off and running. Plymouth's styling was still mundane in 1968, opposite. Some competitors already offered decals and wings. Still, Plymouth's body softened some, as outward curves appeared where scallops had been the first year.

street Hemis, these included a heater, but air conditioning was not available.

If air conditioning seems an odd variable in the muscle car equation, calculate quickly the motivation for offering a pseudo-drag-race car in a convertible version. With about 80 extra pounds added for chassis reinforcement, the car couldn't win. And it cost $260 more!

Furthermore, while the car's exterior styling was subtle, subtlety did not always sell in the muscle car sixties. This was the time of Pontiac's first GTO Judges. Decalcomania had struck the design studios (and the assembly line personnel had nearly struck the plants over the additional handwork required). The more visual and graphic the lines and colors, the more appeal the car generated among young buyers attracted to shiny baubles. At this, Plymouth failed. Yet the car was undeniably the fastest of the muscle contenders. Even the convertible.

Just before the 1968 model introduction, Plymouth analyzed the marketplace for the muscle car buyers, and the results targeted its cars more accurately. Despite lower income, by sheer numbers the cruisers represented the largest of five groups of potential buyers. High styling and low price meant most, even if performance was sacrificed.

Next up were executive hot rodders. They could afford high performance but generally required corresponding style.

Next along were the enthusiast racers, buyers who danced at the country club Friday nights and waltzed at the strip Saturdays. Appearance mattered most: looking as though it was fast meant it was fast.

Hard-core amateur racers came next. For them, the car body merely kept the wind off their faces and held all the pieces together.

For the executive hot rodder, the 426 ci Hemi was what mattered most. Even with a heavier convertible, he could still beat the guy in the office down the hall who drove a Pontiac GTO. Satellites were up, above. Telstar beamed television and a few, expensive telephone calls to and from Europe. In the late sixties, Hemi domes under the hood were far more prevalent than dome-shaped antennas in the American backyards. The 1968 GTX may have been Chrysler's biggest selling Hemi convertible ever, opposite: 36 were made. This amounted to slightly less than a quarter of all Hemi convertibles produced from 1966 to 1971.

In 1967, the GTX Hemi was undeniably the fastest of the muscle car contenders—even the convertible

At the top sat the professional racers. By their choices, they influenced uncountable numbers from the other four groups.

So there it was. If the pros raced Hemis, if the Hemi GTX convertible looked acceptable to the country club membership board yet beat the GTO convertibles, the choice was simple. Even if you couldn't get air.

1968 Chevrolet Corvette L-88 427 convertible
1969 Chevrolet Corvette L-88 427 convertible

The Hiss Of The Snake

From behind the wheel, the Corvette sounds like a snake.

This is not heresy. The sound is even more apparent than the solid lifters' clattering and the exhaust's ponking. Some 850 cfm of God's own air is being sucked out of the atmosphere and down inside the 427. The engine hisses, expectantly. In a snake, a hiss is a threat, a warning; for the aluminum-headed big-block, it's business as usual.

Corvette cockpits have the cramped feel of a CL-41 jet fighter trainer. The steering wheel crowds against a tall driver's thighs; another inch or two of seat travel would be a luxury. But these were race cars, none too thinly disguised. The view from the driver's seat reflects clarity of purpose: everything is visible, accessible. A huge tachometer and speedometer fill the view below the horizon. Above the large dials and the thin steering wheel, the view is channeled partly by the big hood bulge, partly by the Colorado-foothills rise of the wheelwells.

The Ventura County Fire Department auctions off obsolete fire trucks, lined up here near their training facilities for inspection. The red 1969 L-88 was not the fire chief's car.

The clutch engages more gently than expected. It is progressive, heavy, but a linebacker's leg muscles are not needed. And as road speed increases, the hiss coming from that dark air scoop cavern subsides beneath the big-block's mechanical noises. To lever the gearshift up to first, to reach over to third, is a

stretch; each time, your arm passes over a Chevrolet tag admonishing you to keep the tank filled with 103+ octane fuel—Sunoco 260 in the days of this engine. Racing fuel, then and now.

This is the kind of car, like the Baldwin Motion Chevelle that came after it, that goes a long way to encouraging irresponsible behavior on the public streets.

The L-88's acceleration enhances that impression. The engine noise never really intrudes. It's quiet enough, in fact, to let you hear when the rear tires break loose, when they start to shriek.

You can feather the gas coming through a turn and play the steering wheel like a skilled fly fisherman looping out quarter-ounce monofilament before noiselessly dropping the fly. Here, noisily, the car straightens out or drastically overcorrects if you slack off in your driving duties.

The L-88 Corvettes are enthusiastic drivers' cars, frisky, in a word, almost too much fun

44

With scarcely a wasted line and such a pinched waist, Bill Mitchell could have drawn for pin-up calendars. Corvette sold 116 of these L–88s, less than 50 were convertibles such as this. The L–88 427 cast-iron V–8 produced 430 hp in its street trim and gulped in air through a 950 cfm Daytona four-barrel, opposite. Simply uncorking the engine through headers jumped the power up to more than 500 hp.

compared with, say, a 427 Cobra. The real snake is an aim-and-stab (and hang on) automobile. It is brutal, whereas the L–88s are refined, controllable, drivable.

Despite GM's corporate adherence to the AMA ban on auto racing, everyone knows that Chevrolet was serious about its L–88 Corvettes being racers. But there's serious and then there's serious.

Corvette serious was smart marketing. Specifications rated the L–88 engine at 5 fewer horsepower than the L–71s and L–89 engines, at 430 hp compared with 435 hp for the latter two. Yet when unplugged, fitted with 2½ inch headers and water-main-sized pipes (available over the counter at dealership parts departments), the power output jumped to at least 500 hp, and reports of 580 hp before engine modification were not uncommon. Yet for a car whose warranty coverage was largely "at dealer discretion," the decision to advertise it as not the most powerful kept away the indulged sixteen-year-old children of wealthy parents.

Corvette serious was no radio (unshielded transistorized ignition popped the spark better but would have made the radio unlistenable anyway), and no heater in 1967 (it was included in 1968 and 1969; state vehicle code regulations required window defrosters), no power steering, no air conditioning (be serious!), a 12:1 compression ratio, no shroud on the radiator fan.

Corvette serious replaced the standard cross-flow radiator with an aluminum version that was 20 ci larger and 14 pounds lighter. A fan shroud acted like a funnel in low-speed traffic and sucked more air through the radiator, but at racing speeds, it actually would have limited airflow. Of course, the shroud was also available through the parts counter.

Corvette serious meant that heavy-duty brakes were part of the L–88 package. Certain items were mandatory options when ordering the car, and these included two brake packages. One was vacuum power brakes; the other, known as J56, was heavy-duty brakes. The heavy-duty brakes were purely a racer option and were actually a drawback on the street. At low engine speed, in stop-and-go traffic, for example, vacuum boost was inadequate and braking capacity was limited. The J56 brakes required high pedal pressure and used much harder pads that grabbed best when very hot. Slow driving cooled the brakes too much.

Corvette serious meant that no automatic choke was fitted. A manual choke was available (again, see the parts department). Depending on perspective, the cold start procedure was either vastly entertaining (to local fire buffs) or a genuine struggle (to the owner). Because of the open-chamber intake manifold, the fuel was vaporized virtually at the carburetor. Keeping a cold engine running, forget idling, meant constantly blipping the throttle. The engine would spit back; to get the flame back into it, more throttle was required, which pumped more fuel onto the fire. A vicious circle, to say the least.

Corvette serious, to Zora Arkus-Duntov, meant the use of larger tires for racing applications. Arkus-Duntov wanted fender flares fitted at the factory. But the mechanisms that moved the car around the assembly line precluded factory installation. The flares ended up shipped in plastic, sometimes on the passenger seat, otherwise available through the parts department.

Corvette serious also led to fantastic rumors—for example, that L–88s had no passenger seat and couldn't even be ordered with

This was the kind of car that went a long way to encouraging irresponsible behavior on the public streets. Bill Mitchell blended his Mako Shark styling with Zora Arkus-Duntov's serious engineering and produced a street car of desire. On this page, register the car with the local police before you could license it? That was one of many rumors about the L–88s. Advertising conservatively rated the cast-iron 427s at 430 hp. Perhaps if the real power were known, police would have wanted them registered. Buy a pumpkin, it sits on the passenger's lap, opposite. The Sting Rays had no trunk: Arkus-Duntov didn't plan the L–88 as anything other than a pure race car. The cockpits had nowhere near the room of fire trucks. Reminiscent of a cramped jet fighter, their performance was closer to the jet, too. Like the jets, the instrumentation was excellent. Unlike both fire trucks and fighter jets, there was no radio.

one; that the car was uncarpeted, clad in vinyl mats like a police car or worse, plain, resembling a NASCAR stocker; that you had to have written clearance from local law enforcement before you could take delivery. All were false, but all were foundations of the L–88 legend.

For three years, Chevrolet offered the L–88 package. Production figures demonstrate the company's success at downplaying the availability. In 1967, Chevy sold 3,754 L–71s (the triple-carbureted cast-iron 427s) and only twenty L–88s. In 1968, with the beautiful new Bill Mitchell, Mako Shark inspired lines, sales of L–88s soared to eighty cars. A heater was now available, no doubt swelling sales. But the L–71 and L–89 sold 3,522, about forty-four times as many.

For the 1969 model year, Chevrolet added the M40 three-speed Turbo Hydra-matic automatic transmission to the powertrain. By the end of 1969, another sales surge spilled 116 L–88 cars out onto the roads and tracks. Yet the L–88 remained Corvette's best-kept secret.

For 1970, the 427 was bored out to 454 ci. The L-code engines picked up another letter, an S, and two versions were planned. One was a 390 hp engine, the LS–5, and 4,473 were sold. The other was to be the LS–7, successor to Arkus-Duntov's L–88. It was to produce 460 hp and to cost $3,000, the same as the limited-production aluminum 427, which appeared in only two ZL–1 street Corvettes in 1969.

But the LS–7 never made it. The legacy was interrupted. Corvette had introduced the 350 in 1969, to replace the 327, and in its hottest version, the LT–1, it produced 370 hp.

In 1971, a whole new legacy began. Chevrolet introduced its ZR–1 and ZR–2 Corvettes, with the small-block LT–1 and 454 ci, 425 hp LS–6 engines, respectively. Zora Arkus-Duntov's racer was back.

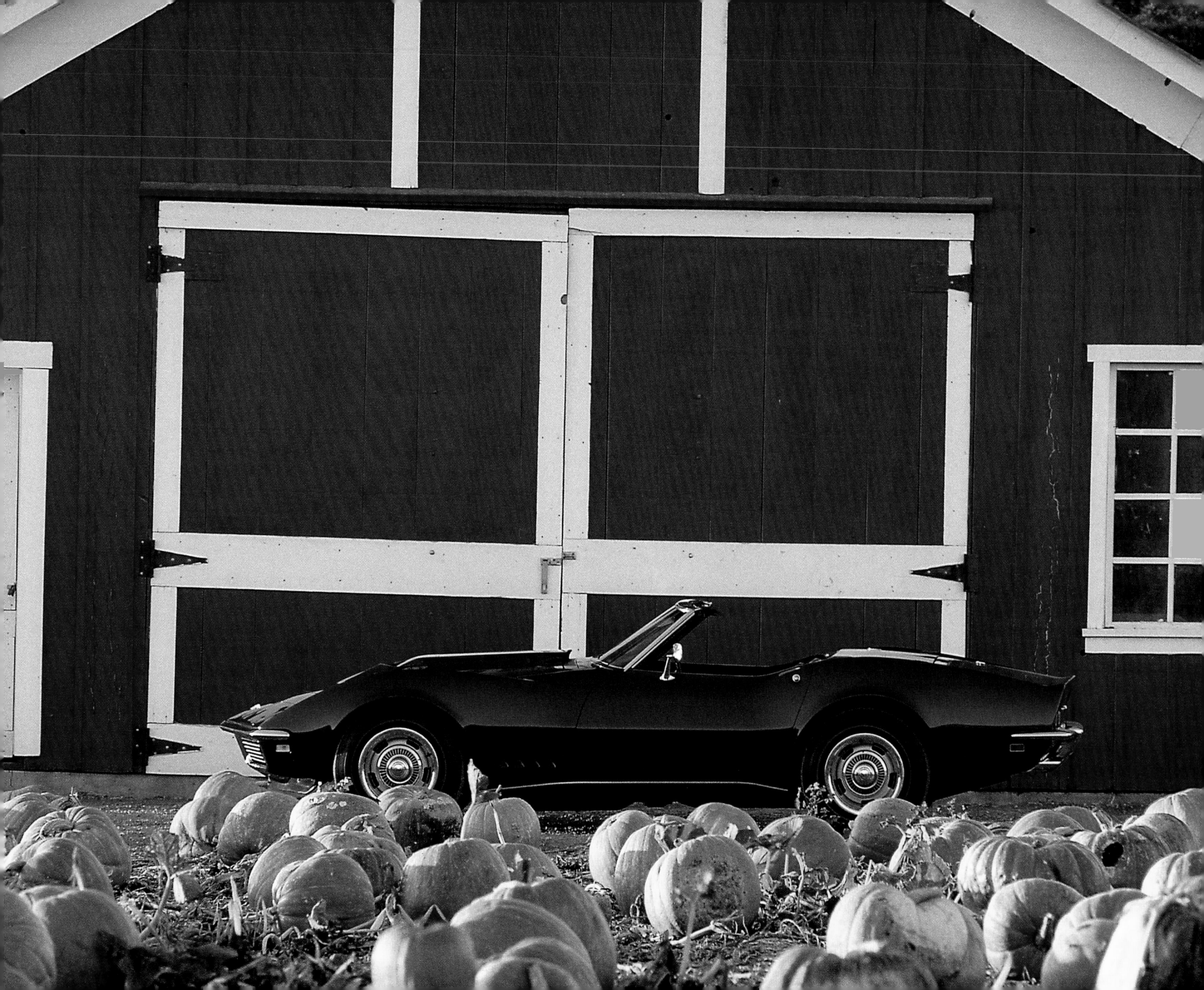

1968½ Ford Mustang GT Super Cobrajet 428 Ram Air

Its Name Didn't Refer To The Horse

Lee Iacocca was not the inventor of the Mustang. Gene Bordinat, Ford's vice president of design, and Don DeLaRossa, chief of advanced design, were the car's creators. The idea, though, probably came from General Motors.

Bill Mitchell, GM's styling chief, took one of Chevrolet's failing economy compacts and jazzed it up for his daughter. A Chevrolet advertising executive, David E. Davis, took a look, was struck by its individual bucket seats, racing-style wheels and special paint, and glimpsed the future. Calling this Corvair the Monza, Davis borrowed it and set it on a stand at the 1960 Chicago Auto Show. The fans went wild.

No longer seen as odd looking or unconventional, the Corvair had become a sporty-looking family car. Davis advised, "Sell it," and advertised it aggressively. Buyers stood in line, and paid list price and more to get one.

By this time, Ford's own product planners, seeing a GM victory snatched from the jaws of

Not all horses are mustangs and this Mustang wasn't named after a horse. Andalusian horses originally come from southern Spain and become pure white at maturity; the Mustang was originally named in honor of the World War II P–51 fighter but a misunderstanding put the wild horse on the grille.

defeat, also saw a great-looking package that was selling as fast as it could be built. But Bordinat and DeLaRossa saw the same possibilities if they installed their own 289 ci engine

into the new Falcon chassis and surrounded it with a two-seater body. Invoking a classic motif to create a new style, they gave the car a long hood and small trunk.

Shown the car in late 1961, Lee Iacocca had glimpsed the future too, and he liked it. From the start of his career, Iacocca's genius had been his ability to sell cars. This car's long-hood, short-deck proportion appealed to his love of the early Continentals, and he took to the new sporty car as if it were his own prodigy. Knowing the first sale he had to make was to Henry Ford II, he did his homework.

Iacocca recognized the postwar babies who were growing into purchasing age. Graduating college, they were moving into the job markets with larger salaries than ever before, a result of the Eisenhower boom years. He took the new car, stretched it just enough to add a small back seat and cannily arranged a car show for Henry Ford II in early 1962. Each of arch-rival Chevrolet's models was matched up opposite Ford's. A gaping hole faced the Monza

for the youth market, which Iacocca argued was expanding quickly. A bright red clay model was rolled out, and the first sale was made.

A target launch date was set: April 1964, the opening of the New York World's Fair. Iacocca motivated his troops. A name was chosen: Mustang, to honor the legendary high-performance World War II fighter—though the misconception that it meant the horse didn't hurt; either was as American as apple pie and both suggested fast movement.

Priced right, its timing was exceptional. The US economy was strong, and Congress was on the eve of enacting a tax cut. Within weeks of introduction, Ford devoted a second and a third plant to Mustang production.

The success of the car was not only its looks but also its distinction as the first modular car. By specifying what you wanted from an extensive list of options, you built a car to suit your own needs—and personality. This was Iacocca's innovation. He took a good basic car and added the bells and whistles, the quick and easy options that not only added to the car's appeal but put real profit into both the dealer's and the manufacturer's pockets. Hundreds of thousands got the car they wanted, and Iacocca got the ride he wanted—to Glass House, Ford's corporate tower, as the forty-year-old vice president of cars and trucks, the number three position in the corporation.

By 1968, Mustang had eclipsed the Corvair but again felt a Chevrolet nipping at its

A single 735 cfm Holley four-barrel rammed fuel down the throat of this big-block. The little notchback would hit 106 in the quarter-mile on the skinny tires of the sixties. Bucket seats were part of the Mustang mystique from the first. Full instrumentation came with the GT package, opposite.

heels. Camaro introduced bigger and hairier engines and more options. Ford responded by upping the ante and offered its already-legendary 427. Pricey, at $622, and essentially a racing engine designed for its best performance at higher engine speeds, it wasn't exactly what the customer wanted in a street machine. But on the car's fourth birthday in April 1968, the 428 Cobrajet was introduced, bringing with it a host of chassis and suspension modifications to take advantage of the power and not be disadvantaged by the weight.

Ford rated—make that *under*rated—the engine at a modest 335 hp. But the conservative reading, probably low by 100 hp, had benefits. Insurance rates were lower than for the engine's 425 hp competition. And Ford virtually annihilated its competition in Super Stock class. Available only in the Mustang GT, the Cobrajet engine essentially fitted the 427's low-rise heads to the 428 Galaxie engine, and gave it a Ram Air induction system through a functional hood scoop. Front suspension was strengthened, rear suspension was modified and Goodyear's Polyglas tires made their premiere on this Mustang.

Introduced in mid 1968, its sales were slim, something like 2,800 engines total, with Shelby Mustang GT500s included in the count. A closer estimate counts around fifty 428SCJ notchbacks produced. The engine was available through the 1970 model year.

The Super Cobrajet 428 was only available in GT package Mustangs. The engine was a $420 option over the 289 ci V–8. Less than 60 were sold. Opposite, Ford designers Gene Bordinat and Don DeLaRossa resurrected a classic styling motif for the Mustang. Throughout the thirties, long hoods and short rear decks had suggested style, grace, speed and power.

The idea for the Ford Mustang probably came from General Motors

1969 Chevrolet Camaro Baldwin Motion Phase III 427

Tow Bars And No Tach Still Written On Dealer Invoice

It sounds like a race car, it looks like a race car. The sound *and* the look. That L–88 style race hood held in place by four clips. The Corvette side-mount exhausts. And the rear wing: not the usual little ducktail spoiler from the other '69s. And tow-bar bolts . . .

Now that's the clue: tow-bar bolts. This was a racer. Had to be. Yet . . .

Look at the interior. That's hound's-tooth cloth, top-line option, class. Slip in behind the wheel. Notice the 120 mph speedometer and the odometer showing only 5,990.6 miles. A glance out the windshield shows that most of

Motion and Baldwin got together to provide enthusiasts a faster car than any manufacturer could offer. Sold through the Baldwin dealership, these street and strip racers even had limited warranty protection. This was the most fully optioned Baldwin Motion Camaro known. A tow bar, no front bumper and freewheeling hubs made getting to the racetracks as easy as racing the backroads. A Corvette-style air induction hood and an Oldsmobile rear wing added style.

the view is blocked by the huge air induction hole. A gigantic flat Mr. Gasket air cleaner lurks in the dark inside there, like some small spaceship waiting for instructions.

A short arm's reach forward delivers the Hurst cue ball to hand. Above it, the Sun gauge package confirms the silence. No amps, no oil pressure, no water temperature. No engine noise to interrupt the quiet; just contemplate the nature of this car. Because in spite of all the other visual clues, cues that say this had to be a race car, there is no tachometer.

OK, sure, maybe this guy was good, one of the few, the proud, the brave who could tell engine revs by ear, by the seat of his pants through that hound's-tooth check.

Twist the key, though, and blow that theory into the next county.

The passenger laughs just as the engine pocka-pockas into life. There are two grab rails for him, one on the door, the other directly in front of his knees. He's figured it out:

No, this was not a race car; this was meant to scare mortals into their next life. That's what this car was about.

The headers coming off the cast-iron 427 deliver a nice pop sound right into the cabin. All race car, sure enough. Turn it on, jump on it. It leaps up and takes off. The sound surrounds the car. It's up front, inside, alongside and behind. Surely a race car. Busy noises, lots of clatters: solid lifters clicking away like a clock gone crazy in fast motion.

The clutch, the linkage, the shifts themselves are forceful. Stiff. Pony cars were supposed to take your girl to the country club dance on Friday night, to the strip on Saturday night and to church on Sunday. Not this car. The Friday night date was two six-packs in the garage, preparing for Saturday night. And they'd stop church and pray for themselves on Sunday if this monster roared into the parking lot.

Yet the confusion persists. Acceleration abounds, but it's more even, steady acceleration than with the Motion Phase III Chevelle. Both rate 500 horses. But at the end of the strip, a chance encounter with a hairpin bend or fast sweeper in this Camaro wouldn't signify the end of life as we know it. As though the car itself understands that it should go fast straight, but maybe it keeps wondering whether it couldn't go faster around the bends, too.

The cam, the kick from opening the Holley's water-main-sized barrels, is so much

A quarter-mile took only 11.4 sec.; at the end, the Camaro was doing 120 mph, opposite. Performance like this did not come cheap. The Baldwin Motion Phase III Camaro sold for $9,330 in 1969. Motion Performance installed the L–72 cast-iron 427 ci engines, replacing factory-ordered 396s. With the 950 cfm Holleys, Motion's engines produced 500 hp and guaranteed the mid 11 sec. quarter-mile times.

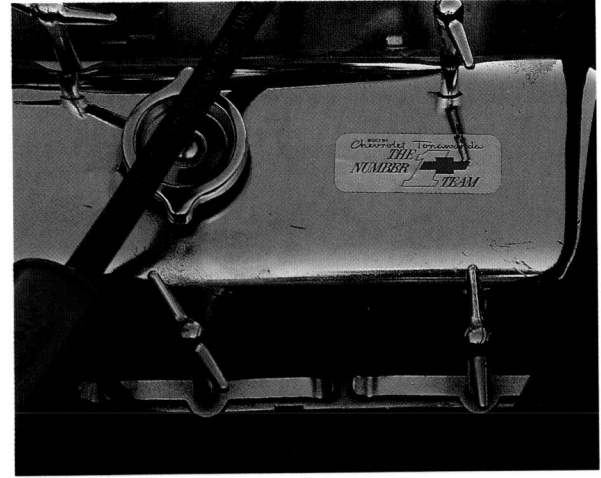

The cast-iron blocks were built at Chevrolet's Tonawanda, New York, engine plant. The engines arrived in crates. They were then blueprinted and dyno-tested before being installed. Pony cars were conceived to take your girl to the country club dance on Friday night and to the strip on Saturday night. Not this car. The Friday night date was two six-packs in the garage, preparing for Saturday.

"I had so much fun with that car. I satisfied every need I ever had with that car"

"He wanted the ultra-lightweight fiberglass hood and he wanted a Pontiac-style hood-mounted tach. It just wouldn't work. So with no tach, Joel Rosen, Motion's founder, fitted the car with a rev-limiter."

Johnson continues, filling in more blanks: "They did race it down there. After all he'd ordered the tow bar and freewheeling hubs. And, a 4.56 rear end is really too mean to get out and drive on the road. But you know he did that too. He was just a young fellow who really liked fast cars."

Irigoyen spent $9,330, but never bothered to remove the window sticker. And when he grew tired of the car, after only 5,400 miles, he never bothered to get rid of it either. Because his wife never cared for her Chevelle, Irigoyen gave it to his right-hand man.

So in the end, paradox explained, it's no less intriguing.

Johnson knows that best of all, too. "I've had nineteen Camaros. And I've seen every last Motion Camaro in existence and there's only five real ones. I had so much fun with that car. I satisfied every need I ever had with that car. And I think Irigoyen just had to have it because it was so hot."

1969 Chevrolet Corvette Baldwin Motion Phase III 427

Joel Rosen's Saturday Night Special

The car squats. Hunkered down in the nose, poised, ready to spring. It defiantly sports different-sized wheels and tires front and rear. Its parts look slightly unmatched, inappropriate to the whole, not of a piece. It suggests some scruffy rag picker, albeit brightly clad, who's taken shoes from one place, trousers from another and a jacket from a third; the colors match, but it still isn't a suit.

But twist the key and settle all doubt. Whatever sort of kit car Corvette this may resemble, when its workday begins, no doubt lingers about the purpose of this odd beast.

If you knew enough and had the motivation, you could have ordered this Corvette from the Baldwin Auto Company on Long Island. A lesser car would have been delivered not to you but to Joel Rosen's Motion Perfor-

The Baldwin Motion Phase III Corvette does not even look at rest when it is at rest. Its nose-down attitude has it poised like a track runner in the starting blocks, ready to spring.

mance, a speed shop just up the road. There, much more was done than merely mismatching cosmetics.

Joel Rosen founded Motion Performance in 1957, but it wasn't until late 1966 that he proposed to Baldwin Chevrolet a collaboration. Rosen's success as a road and drag racer—some thirty world's records by the time he quit—lent credence to his idea.

Rosen put it simply: "The idea was to allow the people to buy a brand new hot rod from a dealer. We used to tout the fact that we could give them a street machine that would run in the elevens. That's why we'd run our car the way we'd sell the package."

Motion's package exchanged cast-iron bits for cast aluminum. Three-barrel carburetors were replaced with enormous four-barrels. Suspensions were diddled with, transmissions transformed, bodies flexed and bulged.

Rosen explained: "If a guy's already buying a special car and he doesn't get what he

wants from a dealer . . . if the dealer can't go far enough, we wondered why not? Why not give him everything he might want? So we were the first out there to put everything on a car a buyer could want and still sell it through a dealer. That was our proposal to Baldwin. We developed a standard package but we also had a catalog."

The full catalog Phase III package and options represented no small investment, some $7,672 in this case, but Rosen's staff of twenty gave you back good value. The Corvette appears more menacing than any other production Corvette ever built. Perhaps it's because this car does not look at rest even when it's shut off, when all its busy mechanicals are silent.

From the rear, the car looks gutted, debauched, as though something has been forcibly removed. It's those giant mufflers, the ones Chevrolet assigned to fit snugly into the rear quarter panels and fill that space; they're gone. Hollow space remains, that job filled now

65

by side pipes that barely dampen the thunder. So the back looks gaunt, and offensive. . . .

Lurking in the dark like some hunchback, this Corvette's sole purpose seems to be the removal, by force of speed, of pink slips from unsuspecting naifs. This car is like the mugger, the thug who hits you and runs away faster than you can in your dazed state. As necessity sometimes teaches young men to prowl, to steal your purse while they beg you for spare change, the lesson they teach you in return is to walk carefully and choose your battles wisely. Perhaps another value received from Rosen's service was teaching boys the ways of the world. And a racing skill to survive.

In the end, the success of any racer, Joel Rosen or his paying proteges buying Motion products, is due in equal parts to the driver's skill and the machinery's strength and reliability. Joel Rosen and Baldwin Auto Company produced many fewer than 1,000 Phase III cars in all varieties. But as with most street crime, the accounts of survivors sometimes get exaggerated. And by description, the perpetrators become legendary.

The full Phase III package included the cast-iron L–72, the same 427 ci engine in the Baldwin Motion Camaro. The 950 cfm Daytona four-barrel hid under a giant Mr. Gasket air cleaner. Motion Performance experimented with transistorized ignitions, eventually using them on all conversions. Opposite, fat tires, flared fenders, side-mounted exhaust pipes and 500 hp on tap at the smash of the foot to the firewall. The nose-down stance was not an optical illusion—it was Motion's intention, the better to enhance weight transfer.

"The idea was to allow the people to buy a brand new hot rod from a dealer. We used to tout the fact that we could give them a street machine that would run in the elevens"

Seldom had a custom hot rod appeared so stock. But most of Motion Performance's modifications were under the hood. This ultimate night stalker sits on an abandoned quarter-mile stretch of California highway. Opposite, the consummate street racer. Twelve were sold in 1969; less than five exist today.

1969 Dodge Coronet R/T
426 Hemi convertible

Rolling Thunder, Optional At Extra Cost

The exhaust has the rhythmic thud of a drill team doing double time, taking the field at half time. It's the Notre Dame marching band and they're taking no prisoners.

Yet tear yourself away from the sound. This is a driver, this one. Get yourself out there onto Woodward or Whittier or Ogden Avenue, pick up second gear and give it some authority. The back end sashays within the lane markers. The whole band is at work now, but it's a percussion group. Foot into the gas, and the exhaust note leaves the tranquility of South Bend on a fall afternoon and blasts quickly to Da Nang. As the back end comes back under control, the sound is strongly reminiscent of 20 mm automatic cannon fire.

Despite the bright—OK, garish—color, there is some discretion to this Hemi. For instance, you won't get picked up within moments when your mind wanders and the speed momentarily approaches 90 mph. Because while it's bright, it somehow looks too

At 3,800 lb, the Coronet R/T was no lightweight. Still, with Hemi power a gas pedal step away, the quarter-mile took 13.85 sec. at 104 mph—speed not for the faint of heart, nor for the light of pocketbook. By 1969, Chrysler Corporation's new car order forms listed every option except good waves and beautiful weather, opposite. Still, only 10 buyers ordered Hemis in their R/T convertibles. This R/T sold new for $4,892.

big to go this fast this quickly.

Just into fourth, barely realizing your speed, under the guise of trying to identify that cannon sound, you back off as quickly as possible. But you can't hide the grin. Sheepish. Embarrassed.

Perhaps the discretion is in the smoothness with which the 426 Hemi moves this heavy weight to extra-legal speeds. The car handles in a taut, almost stiff manner, but disrupting the impression of maneuverability is the steering. Even parking lot maneuvers remind you of the days you helped your mother by pulling in the wash from the lines stretched between the buildings on pulleys. Just keep pulling.

Yet these cars—in fact, virtually all the cars of the sixties—are uniquely American performance cars. No nimble European sports cars these, more attuned to zipping up narrow cobblestones or dissecting the Alps. The US interstate highway system was a fact of life, taken for granted in many places by the time

this vehicle was in the new car showrooms. And, argue as you might over whyever put a racer engine in a convertible ("too heavy, too expensive..."), Americans had only just heard of OPEC and weren't yet worried. Symptomatic of the times, this was just one more affinity group expressing itself, seeking the national attention and a place on the agenda.

Dodge first offered Coronets in 1965 as its intermediates. Hemi engines were offered in 1966, and the R/T model was introduced for the 1967 model year. For 1968, the body was redesigned and the marketing and sales staffs created The Scat Pack, consisting of the Charger R/T, the Coronet R/T and a Dart GTS. The primary identification was a bumblebee stripe around the back tip of the trunk lid. Styling and marketing got even more outrageous for 1969, with nonfunctional air scoops on the sides of the car and standard equipment with the Hemi engines, functional scoops on the hood tied to a fresh air induction system, the Ramcharger. The revelation of performance styling had come to Chrysler; bells and whistles filled out every top-end market.

So far as the Hemis were concerned, some solid engineering was going on as well. Referred to within Chrysler as B-body cars, the Coronet, Super Bee and Charger coupes were all convertible bodies with a roof fitted on. These were stronger than coupe bodies, and separately welded roof panels stiffened up the

Dodge stylists and product planners created wild color combinations; under the hood was no exception. The large air cleaner in Hemi Orange contrasted vibrantly with the exterior green. Dual tachometers were not an option in 1969, above. The factory tach surrounds the clock in the far left circle. A previous owner preferred an easier-reading aftermarket model. This R/T is the only four-speed model known still on the road.

beast even more to handle the Hemi's massive torque. Another steel plate was welded into the floor. And a slightly larger diameter fuel line pumped gas up to the thirsty Hemi engine.

Dodge Division marketed these cars as affordable street racers. As such, many of them were delivered without power steering, power brakes, even a radio (which might draw who-knows-how-much engine power off the alternator turning under the strain of The Beatles or The Doors).

Yet a radio is definitely the way to go with the heavier convertible. This is a party car, a pickup car. With all its scoops and bulges, it conjures up the beach volleyball player, the

athlete with developed muscles. Big athletes feel at home in a big car like this. And you just forget that, unlike the Barracudas and Challengers to come from Chrysler, this car has loads of space. If they could pack twenty-some skinny intellectuals into a Volkswagen Beetle, you've got room for the entire varsity squad, or one friend and two long surfboards, or nearly all your girl friends, or about twenty cases of beer—before you even need to move the ice to the trunk.

Functional hood scoops, nonfunctional side scoops and the bumblebee stripe around the trunk were standard identification on all Dodge Scat Pack R/Ts in 1969. This car even has electric windows and an Am-Fm radio—air conditioning was never available with Hemis. Cold air induction through the hood scoops, however, was standard with the Hemi engine. Unlike the Air Grabber scoop, which had to be opened, these scoops fed air through channels with vacuum-operated shutters inside.

1969 Chevrolet Camaro
427 COPO 9561

Public Secret From A Willing Manufacturer

In 1969, it was easy enough to order a muscle car: Just walk around the corner to your dealership, make your choice, pop out your billfold and sign your name on the dotted line. But there were muscle cars and there were muscle cars. Some models had special packages available if you read the fine print at the bottom of the option list. Sometimes you had to know a certain someone to get that certain package. Other cars were limited-production high-performance vehicles that could be ordered through your local dealer. *How* they could be ordered was another matter altogether.

Time warp? Or a homecoming? Back on the final assembly line at General Motors Van Nuys Chevrolet-Pontiac assembly plant, the 1969 COPO leads a line of current Z–28s through final assembly, opposite. The Muncie M–21 close-ratio four-speed connected Chevrolet's Positraction to its 427, right. The big white cue ball sat atop a Hurst linkage. Essentially a factory race car, the interior was as unadorned as the exterior.

During the sixties, Chevrolet accommodated almost any request that could expand its performance reputation. Through Vince Piggins in special products engineering, certain dealers—Fred Gibbs in Illinois, Dick Harrell in Kansas City and Don Yenko in Pennsylvania, for example—took advantage. They marketed (sometimes even under their own names) cars that were available through any other dealer . . . if you knew they existed and how to get them. A prime example of this is the Camaro COPO.

The acronym COPO stands for Central Office Production Order, and cars produced under this heading were different from those built with RPOs, that is, Regular Production Options. The central office was Detroit headquarters. Production orders from the central office usually changed standard production to fit one or more special parts onto any Chevy. Because all COPO orders were processed through Detroit headquarters before being produced, Detroit had to know you—or your

The L–72 produced 425 hp at 5000 rpm. Torque was rated at 460 lb-ft at 4000. This was adequate to launch the 3,400 lb COPO through the quarter-mile in 12.95 sec. at 108 mph. Time to 60 mph was 4.9 sec. Opposite, Central Office Purchase Order No. 9561 specified the installation of a Tonawanda-built L–72 cast-iron 427 ci engine and other nonstandard Camaro parts. Roughly 300 of these were produced in 1969. Composition in cast iron, above. Restoration to perfection.

dealer—for you to get what you wanted.

Tom Hoxie, now western regional manager for Chevrolet public relations, worked at the central office into the early seventies. He explains: "In most car companies there are systems set up especially for the fleet sales people. A buyer could come to us wanting fifty or 100 vehicles with some sort of special equipment on them. We even had a committee for it which would spec out the vehicle, round up the part numbers and figure the amount of time a regular production line would be tied up on this job. They'd set a price and then bid it back to the buyer."

At about this time, Bunkie Knudsen, savior of Pontiac and enervator of Chevrolet, left GM for Ford, and quickly issued a news release announcing that the new Fords, most likely the Boss 429s, were going to kick Chevrolet the length of a drag strip.

Don Yenko had an established and successful reputation as a road racer in Chevrolet-powered cars. His dealership capitalized on his racing successes, and he promoted a limited-edition line of Camaro Yenko Super Coupes.

Back in Detroit, SYC was known as COPO 9561. That order installed the otherwise unavailable L-72 427 ci cast-iron block into a Camaro. As with Fred Gibbs and the ZL-1, other people may have gotten word of Yenko's car and ordered one as well.

Canadian Wayne Scraba was a customer of Piggins' and knew what it took to work the system. "In order to do a COPO, you had to have Engineering approval. Vince was an engineer, and so were the people working with him. So Vince could initiate a COPO."

Tom Hoxie remembers that Vince Piggins, Chevrolet's racing liaison, "being the astute fellow that he was, figured since there was a whole system in place here, he could make this work for the benefit of the company." The whole job had to be very small, certainly not more than 500 or 600 units. "On the other hand there had to be twenty-five or more, because we wouldn't take an order from a single individual who would buy fifty cars if we'd build them the way he wanted them."

Information about the COPO Camaros is sketchy. At year-end, Chevrolet produced build-out sheets, inventories of the number of cars produced and the optional packages selected. The COPOs didn't even make those lists, so hard facts always contain an element of educated guess.

Scraba again: "Bulletins might be sent to dealers announcing mid-year availability but this was a car available outside the RPO list, a list providing more than 100 variables and twenty-some color options itself. Chevrolet

built 201 for Don Yenko. Educated guesstimates count another 300, but Chevrolet has documentation that nearly 1,000 of the engines were produced with Camaro-use codes."

Hoxie figures that if the truth were known, Piggins had them all sold before production ever started. "He'd sit down and put together a package, then get out his phone list. He'd call up his dealers, the group he knew were performance oriented and ask them 'If I can produce this car with these options for so much, would you be interested?' Occasionally the public heard about it and asked their own dealer, but likely as not they got 'Huh?' If they

During the sixties, Chevrolet accommodated almost any request that could expand its performance reputation

ever got to Piggins, they might have gotten the car, or it might have been sold out already."

Buyers wanting stylish graphics or more elaborate interiors went to Yenko, or to Baldwin if even more performance was the goal. Scraba paints in more of the picture: "Those cars were not COPOs—not even Yenkos until 1969; the factory engines were 396s which Nickey or Berger, Dana or Baldwin replaced after delivery. Some of those cars were strong on graphics too." It does seem that many COPO buyers kept their cars simple and unadorned.

So by the time Bunkie Knudsen issued the threat, Piggins had already imagined the iron-block 427 L-72 engines in Camaros. Yenko had

asked him if the factory could install the 427s, and then he asked them to keep the project under wraps. It left Yenko with an exclusive product, and he put on his stripes and sold it for Piggins.

That may explain the scarce information. The limited space in magazines was often devoted to those who made their products known and available. Editors looking for splashy color covers for newsstand sales were unimpressed by harmless stock appearances. And COPO owners may have appreciated that same understated look.

Especially when they were baiting the driver in the car alongside them.

The COPO packages came from General Motors fleet operations, opposite. Through special products engineering, almost any request that would further Chevrolet's performance reputation was accommodated. It only took engineering approval. Chevrolet installed the L-72 427 ci engines in COPO Camaros, above, unlike Baldwin Motion's aftermarket creations, which replaced stock 396s. This was the factory version of Don Yenko's SYC, and was available through any other dealer who knew enough to order it.

1969 Chevrolet Camaro Yenko/SC 427

1969 Chevrolet Chevelle Yenko/SC 427

Any Chevy, Any Color—So Long As It's Fast

Don Yenko spent a great deal of the sixties opening people's eyes.

In 1962 and 1963, Yenko took SCCA's B/Production class championships driving a Corvette. It's possible that those victories opened some eyes at Ford Motor Company, and they may have given Carroll Shelby a new job.

In 1967, racer Jerry Thompson campaigned a race-prepared Corvair, the Yenko Stinger, to win the D/Production class national championship. History did not record the reaction of Ralph Nader.

Earlier in 1967, Chevrolet Division introduced the Camaro. Initially the biggest engine available was the L-78, a 396 ci Turbo Jet producing 375 hp. It was neither big nor powerful enough for Don Yenko.

Yenko owned a Chevrolet dealership in Canonsburg, Pennsylvania, roughly twenty-five miles down the road from Pittsburgh. He started Yenko Sports Cars in the same location in 1965, developing the company to focus

Don Yenko's more prevalent muscle car, the Camaro SYC, sold 201 copies in 1969. Yenko added his own graphics and badges, as well as trim and instrumentation to the otherwise stock COPO Camaro. Yenko Sports Cars was founded in 1965 as an offshoot of the Chevrolet dealership in Canonsburg, Pennsylvania, outside Pittsburgh.

on performance owing to his racing successes. His racing connections gave him access to Zora Arkus-Duntov and his Mark IV Mystery engine, the L-72. It was Yenko's thought to

install these cast-iron 427 ci engines in SS396 package Camaros.

Fifty-four of the 427s found their way into Camaros and onto the street in the first year. Other dealers performed similar transplants, but Yenko expanded on the theme by including aftermarket wheels and headers, and additional instruments.

Stewart-Warner gauges were optional, mounted below the dash to provide engine status information in the early 1969 cars, and these worked in concert with a Stewart-Warner 8000 rpm tach. Unfortunately, rather than passing a solid-wire lead from the engine to the tach, Yenko's selection used a transistor unit through the firewall. It was unreliable, and many owners simply raced by the seat of the pants. Giving some perspective to such seat-of-the-pants appraisals was another COPO item, the 140 mph police pursuit speedometer.

In 1968, Yenko sold sixty-four cars. Sensing the possibilities for additional profitability

As with Yenko's Chevelle automatics, the Muncie M–40 three-speed floor unit replaced the factory column shifter. Of the 201 Camaros built, only 30 used automatics. The 427 ci engine used in the automatic transmission versions had hydraulic valve lifters and was rated at 425 hp. Yenko did not have separate engine decals made, and used the solid-lifter decal on all engines. Front air dam, rear spoiler, air induction hood: all were part and parcel of the Chevelle package, opposite.

opening before his very own eyes—he was, after all, a successful dealer-businessman—he went up to Detroit to talk with his racing buddy Vince Piggins. They discussed and solved the matter of Yenko's getting out of the car manufacturing business and Chevrolet's expanding to pick up the slack. Through a Central Office Purchase Order, Piggins would

specify the car built the way Yenko wanted it. Upon delivery, Yenko's service personnel would then paste on the side graphics, install the aftermarket gauges and move it out.

Piggins went for the idea. For 1969, Piggins' Product Promotions authorized installing as many L–72 Camaros at the factory as there were orders. Yenko started out with 100, but the orders didn't stop. The final count for 1969 included 171 four-speed transmissions and thirty automatics, a total of 201 cars. The automatics were delivered with the milder 410 hp engine. The transmissions' shifters were delivered on the steering column. Yenko punched a hole in the floorboard and angled a Hurst Dual-gate floor-shift three-speed into position.

The four-speed version rated an extra 40 hp. The difference was owed to automatic cars using the hydraulic-lifter version of the engine, where the four-speed engines used solid lifters. Both versions shared an aluminum intake manifold, an 11:1 compression ratio and factory headers. Muncie's M–21 (Yenko felt the M–22 was too noisy) and a choice of rear axle ratios, all with limited-slip, took care of under-the-hood concerns for the four-speed. And Yenko's staff took care of transforming the exterior into a Yenko Super Camaro.

1969 Dodge Charger Daytona 426 Hemi

180 Mph Right Out Of The Showroom

Architects of the sixties would have loved this thing. They would have approved mightily of its form-follows-function purity though they might have lamented its asymmetry. Its low, pointy nose . . . its cathedral-high wing . . . but most irreconcilably, its driver sitting off to one side, not perfectly centered, would have offended the balanced eye.

Sculptors would have loved this too, had they seen one. The sensuous undulations that might have put off the architect would have spoken to the sculptor.

For this most sculptural of the muscle cars was also the most emblematic of its function dictating its form. By virtually all accounts, it was the most outrageous car ever to leave an auto maker's factory destined for the street. Never mind that it was born of a necessity to meet some racing rule maker's quota. Described by Dodge stylist John Herlitz as "world class ugly," it was design beyond bold. It was outlandish.

It also functioned so exquisitely at its

The significant aerodynamics yielded the most outrageous styling to visit America's streets. The Daytona's rear wing was needed to counter the lift created by its bullet nose; the wing's height in turn resulted from the need to open the trunk. The wing was bolted through to the rear frame members. Racing-type fuel filler and the wide Daytona bumblebee stripe around the rear typified Dodge Scat Pack graphics.

prime task that in prime task dress, it claimed and held for thirteen years the closed-course speed record, at 201.104 mph. In a wilder moment of advertising hyperbole, Bobby Isaac, the NASCAR driver who achieved the

record, allowed as how the car's stability was such that any driver could go out and run 180 mph right out of the showroom.

"We ran our first test on the day they landed on the moon, July 16," remembers Gary Romberg, Chrysler's former aerodynamicist. Chrysler Space Division had won the contract for the space booster in 1963, and he had worked on it. At least one of his projects soared that day. "We were just building the first race cars and production cars. We were out at Chrysler proving ground that day, and our first track tests were not very good."

Dodge engineers put in months of wind tunnel testing at Wichita State University with scale models to come up with a method of beating Ford's NASCAR entries. All the manufacturers ran 426 or 427 ci engines. New engine development was not financially feasible for Chrysler, especially for the sake of racing. Drawing paper and wind tunnel time made much more efficient use of available resources.

"We actually had a budget and we didn't. We had all the money we needed to set up the cars and do the work. We had a whole stable of race cars and crews. The money to do that and rent tracks was all there," Romberg recalls. "The money for engineering was on a shoe-string."

A year earlier, Dodge filled in the rough spots on its Charger to cut more cleanly through the super-oval air. The recessed headlights and grille of the production car were moved forward, made flush with the bumper. And the recessed rear window, which created its own turbulence, was brought up flush with the roofline. Thus, NASCAR, requiring that all fixes be regular production, fostered another new car, the Charger 500.

Romberg recalls: "The Daytona project was crash and burn on time. Then late Summer 1969, Charlie Glotzbach ran 202 and 204 with a race car at the proving grounds. He got out of the car and said 'Set up the grandstands right here. This is the best racetrack in the country.'" That was the second time in 1969 that a Romberg project soared.

Ford was set to introduce its NASCAR killer Torino Talladega. The Dodge engineers had retreated to their tunnel and paper; Chrysler's secret weapons were Romberg and physicist John Pointer. A longer, tapered nose sliced the air more cleanly, but it created lift in the bargain. A chin spoiler was slipped in down low to counter the effect somewhat. But it was enough to create serious lift at the back of the car. That was solved with the high wing.

Tunnel tests showed that the bullet nose created 200 pounds of downforce and the wing added 600 more at the rear. Isaac's car slunk close to the track, with its nose even lower. With larger tires filling the wheelwells, reversed air scoops above the front tires

expelled some air pressure and accommodated suspension travel.

Pointer designed in 12 degrees of wing adjustability so racing teams could tune the car for various tracks. The high wing remained up on both road and track cars to provide trunk access for the street.

Romberg laughs when he remembers the ten months with little sleep. "It was fun at the time because we had all this great latitude to do whatever we wanted to do. Bob McCurry was at the top directing us. He was known as Captain Crunch, and he directed us to build a winning race car."

The car made its premiere at Talladega in September 1969. A drivers-versus-track dispute put an unknown, Richard Brickhouse,

into the car, and he frequently topped 190 mph during the race, three times touching 195 mph. It was enough to beat Ford's Talladega namesake.

The NASCAR organization never liked strong winners. Winners interrupted close racing—and jeopardized ticket sales. Romberg remembers different motivations: "Captain Crunch said, 'No excuses. I don't want to hear anything except the applause when we win the Daytona 500.' A lot of drivers had pictures of McCurry on their dashboard. A sign below said, 'Win or Die.'"

Bobby Isaac swept the Daytona's namesake race and went on to win the 1970 season championship. Ironically, his sponsor was Indianapolis-based K&K Insurance, a com-

"No excuses. I don't want to hear anything except the applause when we win the Daytona 500"

In 1969, NASCAR driver Bobby Isaac pronounced the car so stable that any driver could go and run 180 mph straight out of the showroom. Such claims sent insurance companies racing to their rate books. Exactly 503 of these cars were produced to qualify the car for NASCAR. The sight of these on the streets turned heads and stopped traffic; the appearance of the cars on the super ovals led to the 1970 series championship for Dodge.

pany specializing in motor sports coverage. The irony is that although the car's flamboyant looks turned heads even while they put off buyers, the automobile insurance industry damaged Daytona sales most. State Farm Insurance and its competitors' growing dislike of muscle cars resulted in quoted rates of between $500 and $800 per year in 1969 for a single male living in Los Angeles with a clean driving record. A couple moving violations accelerated premiums to $2,000 per year for a Daytona, and by midyear, dealers were dumping the cars for as little as $3,000.

1969 Chevrolet Camaro Z-28 302 Cross Ram

See The USA In A Chevrolet

We're not talking the Dinah Shore road show here. No, this was a show, all right, but it was the Mark and Roger Show. Mark Donohue and Roger Penske were two entertainers who performed regularly on the Sunday afternoon road course circuit. For years, they were the feature act.

But the interesting part of this show tour was its mandatory audience participation. The tour promoter, the Sports Car Club of America, required that the cars Penske managed and Donohue drove be based on current production models, available to the paying public. So for Penske and Donohue to play the tour, Chevrolet Division had to put up at least 200 big ones, cars that is. And that, rather loosely, is how this 1969 Camaro Z-28, and 205 others like it, came to be.

Just as with Mark Donohue's race car, this Z-28 is equipped with Chevy's small-block V-8 with two four-barrel carburetors mounted on a Cross Ram induction manifold. All that length and the extra carburetor created a lot

The Z-28 was Chevrolet's regular production code for its street version of the SCCA Trans-Am racer. More than 20,000 were produced but only 206 were equipped with racer-like four-wheel disc brakes. The Z-28 was happiest when running the twists at racetracks like Riverside International Raceway's Esses, opposite.

of top-end horsepower and little low-end torque. The good news was that the car had greater flexibility near the top of each gear

and a higher top speed; the bad news was that freight trains could accelerate from a standstill faster . . . and perhaps quieter.

Getting off the line required high revs, clutch slippage and then wheel spin. Not bad if you were doing it just once at the start of a 200 mile race but tedious if you were trying to beat the guy in the AMX next to you to the next stoplight. It was possible to do that anyway, because of the other significant feature of this Mark Donohue spin-off: option JL8, doing business as four-wheel disc brakes. That coupled with all the other pieces bolted into this car provided the essence of a season champ.

Front and rear spoilers (with size and location determined by testing from Chevrolet R&D so they worked), stiffer springs and shocks, larger antiroll bars, power steering (ummhmmm!) and a close-ratio four-speed to keep those revs well within the band made this car work quite nicely, thank you very much. Firestone Sports Car 200 tires mounted up on

wide, 7 inch rims gave the car great cornering ability.

A road test at the time concluded that the extra carburetor seemed inconsequential in tight, fast turns; that excess power needed to throw the car into a four-wheel drift was not there, and bending through the turns seemed less dramatic and also less quick. The testers reasoned that all that power sliding was great for the outback dirt track, but it wasted power and scrubbed speed on the asphalt. A check with a clock proved this true; the cars looked neater and ran quicker.

Many more modifications were dreamt up by the Penske crews, Chevy R&D, and chief engineer and driver Donohue himself. But one story typifies Penske and explains an option shown here.

Complaints from other teams were lodged during the time Donohue and Penske ran a car with a vinyl roof in competition. It was common knowledge from years of competing against Penske that he was an innovator and a perfectionist. A careful reading of the rules outlined strict weight limitations on the car. He reasoned that one important place to remove weight would be up high, to lower the center of gravity. There was no rule against that. So weight was reallocated, and the roof was removed and lightened. When the panel was finished, Penske thought it looked rippled and unattractive, so he had it covered with vinyl. His competitors surmised that it was an exotic, superslippery surface or was hiding some illegal material. But for Roger Penske, it was strictly for looks.

Mark Donohue raced a Z–28 for Roger Penske and Sunoco during the 1969 Trans-Am series. The Donohue-Penske effort proved unbeatable and the Camaro won the season. A special instruments option, above, placed the ammeter, temperature, oil pressure and fuel gauges in stacked pods on the console. On the dash, the speedometer and tach filled the big squares above the steering wheel. Heartbeat of the Z–28 was the Cross Ram induction, opposite. Using two 600 cfm Holley four-barrels, the street Z–28 put out 290 hp at 5800 rpm, 290 lb-ft torque at 4200. With maximum power and torque available at high engine speeds, stoplight racing was not the car's strength.

Getting off the line required high revs, clutch slippage and wheel spin. Not bad if you were doing it just once at the start of a race but tedious if you were trying to beat the AMX at the stoplight

95

1969 Chevrolet Corvette ZL-1 427

"600 Hp Sounded Pretty Good To Me"

Jack Cheskaty was tired of getting beaten. Beaten by his friend who drove an L-88. Beaten by another guy who drove a 427 Cobra. Cheskaty raced a fuel-injected 1965 Corvette through 1967 and 1968. Running in NHRA C/Sports class, he was frequently lagging behind. Then he heard about a new Corvette, a ZL-1, with a lot of horsepower.

"It was in one of the old magazines back then," Jack Cheskaty remembers. "One of them picked up some information about this Mystery Porcupine Head. I was racing a 327 ci fuel-injection 1965 coupe... but the big-blocks were just awesome. I finally succumbed." Not knowing much more about the car, he set out to get one.

Cheskaty had heard that the cam was a bit wilder. The dealer in Denver, where he

No badges announced ZL-1. No warnings were issued to the uninitiated. The ZL-1 was produced for NHRA drag racing purposes and never intended for street use, opposite. Yet its first owner drove it home from Salt Lake to Denver.

lived, was little help. Cheskaty had heard that it "breathed a bit better." A dealer in Grand Junction couldn't help, couldn't get him one. Cheskaty began to think that whatever it was, it would be perfect for A/Sports class, "unbeatable," he thought. The dealer in Colorado Springs hadn't even heard of it.

He kept searching: "Six hundred horsepower was reported and that sounded pretty good to me. I started calling around to different zones. Finally I started putting the word out I'd pay the ticket." Cheskaty was an engineer with the Atomic Energy Commission, single and living at home.

A Denver dealer heard that the ZL-1 was to be built but not for private sale. Then a salesman from a dealership in Magna, Utah, a suburb of Salt Lake, called Cheskaty to find out just how serious he was.

The Utah dealer gave him a serial number and Cheskaty sent a $500 deposit by registered mail. With a taste of victory on the tip of his tongue, Cheskaty flew to Salt Lake three

weeks later and got his car. Looking first at the engine, he realized that he had failed to bring a magnet when he saw the block was painted. But with his pocketknife he scratched a bit of the paint off, and he knew aluminum well enough to know aluminum. Then he took it for a short test drive before signing any papers.

"I knew what it was going to cost," said Cheskaty. "I knew it was going to be expensive. I had thought about getting a Hemi 'Cuda. Based on that cost, I figured the Corvette to be a couple thousand more. I just didn't expect it to be that much more. Not four thousand. But you see, by then I was committed. I'd told all my friends about my new hot car and anyway with the NHRA A/Sports class, I thought I had it licked."

He noticed that the car had slightly more than 100 miles on it and suspected that others had taken short test drives as well. The salesman excused it with "Hey you know, the car had to be moved here and there and..." And

Cheskaty wondered if "here and there" was a quarter-mile at a time.

Still, he'd come to buy a car, and as he later described it, the car ran extremely well, turning the tires to smoke easily. So he paid his balance of $9,819, and drove home.

Once home, Cheskaty set about seriously to prepare and run the car before the fall internationals. A friend, USAC Rookie of the Year Woody Walcher, worked with Cheskaty to get some sponsorship. Doug Thorley Headers helped, producing a set for the car; Holley sent a new 1100 cfm carburetor; a local clothing store provided them uniforms; and Dixon Instruments also supported the effort.

The headers and carburetor went on, the

Corvette's cowl induction fitted the air cleaner element into the hood, opposite. The small birdcage atop the 427 aluminum block was not its sole protection. Rated power output of 430 hp matched the cast-iron L-88's. The ZL-1 advantage was 100 lb less weight to move down the quarter-mile. Rarer by far than ZL-1 Camaros, the ZL-1 equipped Corvette is one of only three produced, above. One, a Chevrolet development car, was subsequently destroyed by the manufacturer.

rear axle was changed to a 5.13:1 and wrinkle wall slicks replaced the street Tiger Paws in back. But even before it ran, NHRA changed the rules. It eliminated the class Cheskaty had purchased the car for, and reassigned him to Modified Production.

With his older fuel-injected Corvette, which ran in the low thirteens, as a benchmark, Cheskaty knew what to expect—or so he thought. When he ran the ZL-1 up to 6000 rpm and popped the clutch, the slicks spun. "'So what,' I thought, 'my old car did that.' The slicks started to burn, and again, 'So what, my old car did that, too.' But then the slicks grabbed and it was all I could do to grab on to the shift lever to get second before the tach hit 7000. I knew this was something different."

His first run was mid-twelves, and he was impressed. Over time he pulled two more seconds off that, running better than 130 mph at the end of the quarter-mile. The car didn't see the street again for years.

Rarely has a purpose-built race car seemed so stock. With the exception of a pair of tags on the center console, the ZL-1 looks like any other 427 Corvette. It is those tags and, of course, a glimpse at the aluminum engine that give away the secret.

The AMA race ban kept manufacturers out of racing but did nothing against the guy who dropped a Corvette engine into a family coupe and took it to the strip Saturday night

A tiny plate behind the gearshift identifies the ZL-1 package. A larger sticker warns of the engine's 103 octane requirement. No radio and no heater betray an otherwise completely stock 1969 Corvette interior, above. Opposite, Jack Cheskaty bought this car new. His first run down the strip was an eye-opener. With open exhaust headers and slicks, he ran a mid 12. With practice he got that time down 2 sec. lower and trap speeds up to mid 130, nearly quick enough to stop and wait for his competition.

1969 Chevrolet Camaro ZL-1 427 COPO 9560

Mystery Engine As Secret Weapon

In 1957, the AMA, of which all American auto manufacturers were members, banned its members from racing. General Motors had issued a policy statement that it was not involved in racing, but for some within the company it was not that simple. For people like Zora Arkus-Duntov and divisions like Chevrolet, it presented an enigma. Arkus-Duntov's responsibilities were the high-performance projects, those close to racing. And the only American sports car at the time was Chevrolet's Corvette.

The reality, of course, was far different. The ban kept manufacturers out of racing but did nothing against the private individual who dropped a Corvette engine into a family coupe and took it to the strip Saturday night, or onto the super ovals Sunday afternoon. Under the guise of improving the product, Arkus-Duntov and his staff continued development. And the outsiders continued buying optional products.

Then in 1962, all that changed. Bunkie Knudsen, fresh from reinventing Pontiac Divi-

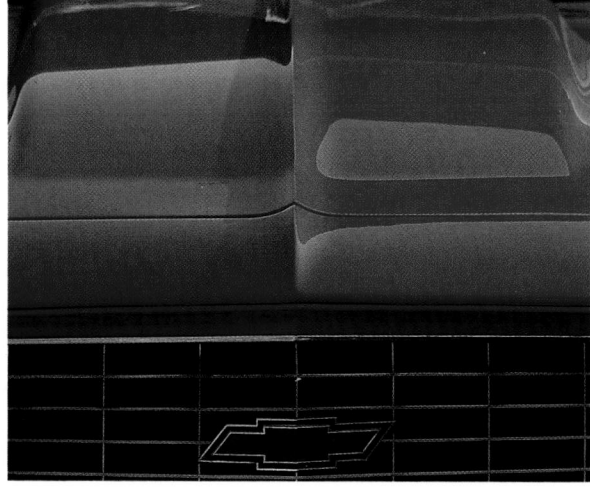

Born of Chevrolet's all-aluminum small-block Can-Am engine, the big-block ZL-1 added $4,160 to the $2,800 base price. The Camaro Sport Coupe, COPO 9560, pulled like a locomotive, opposite. In 1962, Chevrolet engineers were asked to replace the 409 ci engine, the Mark I big-block. The eventual results were the L-36, L-72 and L-88 Mark IV 427s. The ZL-1 aluminum 427 weighed 100 lb less with the same power output.

sion, was promoted general manager of Chevrolet. Among his first acts was to authorize creation of a new engine for the NASCAR series, one to replace the aging 409.

With a clean drawing board and a blank check to fund the job, the assignment was given to Arkus-Duntov and an assistant, Dick Keinath. They set about immediately to remedy some of the breathing problems with the original 409, referred to internally as the Mark I engine. The new one became the Mark II, and owing to the angles at which the valves were seated—26 degrees for intakes but only 16 degrees for exhausts—earned the street name Porcupine Head.

A stroked crankshaft enlarged the engine to 427 ci, a size limit accepted by NASCAR for Pontiac and for Chrysler's new Hemi. People at NASCAR kept the details quiet and rumors erupted over GM's new Mystery engine. The cast-header exhaust system was finished and the engine was ready for testing. It proved fast, producing some 510 hp, and at Daytona in

Only 69 of the ZL–1 Camaros were built. In street trim the 3,300 lb coupes would turn 13 sec., 120 mph quarter-mile runs. With street trim the ZL–1 rated 430 hp at 5600 rpm, 450 lb-ft torque at 4400, opposite. Prepared for NHRA Super/Stock drag racing, with headers and short pipes, something closer to 580 hp was produced. It came standard with the COPO Camaro and could be ordered with the Z–28 or SS options: the air intake was located at its rear, at the base of the windshield, to take advantage of a low-pressure area.

"When the slicks grabbed, it was all I could do to grab on to the shift lever to get second before the tach hit 7000. I knew this was something different"

early 1963, Smokey Yunick's car ran 10 mph faster than the competition until a valve quit. So secret was the Mystery engine that Keinath and another engineer on the project took vacation time to go to Daytona to watch and work.

In April 1963, General Motors reiterated its no-racing rule, adding, "If you do, you're fired." The Mark II had been designed as a racing engine that could be detuned for street use. GM's latest dictum gave birth to a back-door policy. The corporate rule benders got a few completed engines and spare parts out to Yunick and a couple other loyal outsiders. Then, under the guise of production-based applications, work began on a Mark III and its almost-immediate successor, the Mark IV.

Mark II engines lurked around Mount Clemens, Michigan, as development pieces for the Mark IV. The precious few outsiders contributed their experiences as well. By the time the engine reached the public in 1966 as a Regular Production Option (an L-code engine), Roger Penske had even run a couple Mark IVs at Daytona and Sebring in sports car endurance races. The mechanical-valve-lifter version was labeled the L–72 and the hydraulic-lifter engines were L–36s, and the L–88 (limited-production Corvette engine with aluminum heads, a hot cam and a single 4V carb) and L–89 (street version of the L–88) joined the Chevrolet RPO roster.

Ironically, about this time, research and development engineers began to lose interest in the project. The engine was virtually unbeatable; ZL–1 racers ended up in finals against other ZL–1 racers. For 1969, owing to Piggins' efforts, the engine became publicly available, but only two ended up in Corvettes. As COPO 9560, however, the $4,160 option was fitted into sixty-nine Camaros, fifty of which went to Illinois dealer Fred Gibb and Kansas City drag racer Dick Harrell.

As a race engine designed for use with headers and open, short pipes, the all-aluminum V–8 produced 585 hp at 7000 rpm. Nearly the same power was possible from the cast-iron block, but at the expense of another 100 pounds. The real penalty was felt when street-legal exhaust was added: power dropped to 430 hp at 5800 rpm. That penalty added 2½ seconds to a quarter-mile time and cut nearly 20 mph at the traps.

What did those creative R&D engineers get involved with next? In advance of the winds blowing out from Washington, they were directed into exhaust emissions research.

1970 Buick Gran Sport GSX Stage I 455

Wouldn't You Really Rather Have The Silk Purse

Buick left Eisenhower's fifties in mid 1965, GM's last division to join John DeLorean's Pontiac GTO. Five years later, Buick had a credible muscle car. Perhaps the best-kept muscle car secret, it may have been one of the best muscle cars. Every year, Buick's engineers chipped away at its ever-fewer problems so that when 1970 came around, the GSX was closer to DeLorean's *gran turismo* idea than was any other GM product.

Buick Division, it seemed, was caught unaware of the sixties youth market. It had catered to a mature market—one that could also afford its well-built, conservative products. Yet, Buick had introduced the Riviera; at least stylistically, the marque was on the mark.

The Gran Sport started life as a $250 Skylark option. However, it suffered from a problem common with its competition: it was badly balanced and its brakes were abominable. The balance problem affected straight-line performance. With nearly sixty percent of the car's weight over the front wheels, rear wheel

spin was unavoidable. The braking problem was the result of using drums from Chevrolet's compact Chevy II on a car weighing much more and capable of much greater speed.

The 1966 model year brought new skin. Changes under the hood were subtle. The 401 ci nail-valve engine still powered the Gran Sports. Small-diameter intake and exhaust valves shed heat more quickly than did large ones, greatly reducing the risk of burning. Quiet operation, not snorty exhaust, was the Buick hallmark. Yet small valves restricted breathing and ultimately, performance.

For 1967, the changes were welcome and noticeable. The Gran Sport became its own line. Three-speed automatic transmissions and Wide Oval tires performed much better at getting Buick's 340 hp to the ground. The sus-

The 1970 GSX was the result of five years of Buick's steady improvement of a good idea. Nearly 700 were produced. Characterized as a muscle car for the upper crust, it hinted that no one was immune from the pull of horsepower.

Buick conservatively rated its monster 455 ci engine at a modest 360 hp at 4600 rpm, opposite. Torque suggested the truth: 510 lb-ft at 2800. Outside air was inducted through two flush hood intakes into foam-insulated tunnels. This was a serious muscle car effort to Buick. With other GM divisions attacking the streets with a vengeance, Buick's GSX represented the marque admirably. The hood tach and the GSX vibrant paint scheme betrayed its intent, above. The seats, like those in most muscle cars, looked more supportive than they were, above right. A refreshing lack of chrome and restraint in simulated wood marked the interior. A four-speed transmission was offered but most were sold with automatics.

When better automobiles are built, Buick will build them. And here it was, a muscle car for the Junior League

pension, already well liked by magazine writers, got firmed up considerably, with spring rates and roll bar diameters increased by nearly twenty-five percent. Disc brakes were optional. With the 1967 GS400, Buick now had a muscle car worthy of its old advertising claim: "When better automobiles are built, Buick will build them." It was, as one writer theorized, a muscle car for the Junior League.

Times were changing at Buick, but in a typical Buick way: subtly. A new catalog was circulated filled with descriptions strongly suggesting racing. Were Buick's engineers trying to teach Junior Leaguers that going for a pink slip had significance beyond making midnight panty raids on sorority houses?

Mid 1968 options made midnight runs more potent; Stage I and II packages were factory available. Stage I meant 345 hp, and a reworked transmission that traditional Buick owners would immediately return for warranty repair. Stiff shifts, plus special cams, stronger valve springs and ignition modifications, targeted this car to Junior Leaguers' blue-jeans-clad sons. Still a Buick, it was possibly the most civilized of the muscle cars, its level of finish among the highest of any street fighter's. And the best was about to get better.

Cold air arrived in 1969. A new hood plunged outside air directly into the engine and meant nearly a ten percent power increase throughout the entire engine range.

And then came the seventies. New body, new engine, new suspension, new brakes, still-subtle badges, more power, new transmission . . .

Their state-of-the-performance-art was the GS455 Stage I. With this engine, which Buick conservatively (remember, this was Buick) rated at 360 hp, torque was 510 lb-ft: if those Tri-Delts won't give you their pink slips, pull the sorority house walls down! General Motors finally abandoned its 400 ci limit. Marketing demands had won. One of the more reasoned magazine writers mused, ironically and apocryphally, whether this was really the direction US auto makers should be taking.

Mid 1970, Buick took its greatest leap into the muscle car fray. Its own advertising called it a new brand of Buick. Ordinary classic, conservative, subtle styling was gone. Graphics appeared. A rear wing was added. A tachometer grew out of the hood. Yet, remarkably, it was still a Buick. Which meant it still had a level of luxury and finish virtually unmatched on the street or strip.

The old nail-valve-restricted breathing legacy was dean. The 1970 version of the monstrous 455 had tunnel-ported intake and exhaust valves. A high-lift, long-duration camshaft, still-stiffer valve springs and the largest valves Buick ever used nailed the coffin closed. Buick even had Stage II parts available through its dealers. These could propel its silk-swathed luxury muscle car through the quarter-mile in the high elevens: 11.85 at 117 mph to be exact!

Buick walked a tightrope producing the GSX. Even now the interior bespeaks luxury. A four-speed was available, but it is difficult to imagine that many sold. The automatic trans-

mission shifts by a U-shaped bar sliding up and down a bunny hill ski slope of chrome. Comfortably seated behind a big padded wheel, in plush but nonsupportive seats, the view forward is interrupted only by the cowl-mounted tachometer set adrift on the sea of flat black. Almost unnoticeable were two insets for the cold air ram induction.

The car is smooth in all behavior. A bit too nose heavy for twisty roads, but this is not surprising; few street racers cared much for nimble cornering. Yet its Buick heritage is obvious. Its acceleration feels fast, yet little intrudes. The carburetor inhales heavily, the exhaust exhales sonorously, but this is clearly a car built in the continuation of a tradition.

Six years before this, the dowager from Pasadena would have lost her license driving a Superstock Dodge. Cut from the same cloth, her daughter would have loved this GSX. There's no question what her grandson would have thought.

1970 Chevrolet Chevelle SS Baldwin Motion Phase III 454

An Outrageous Toy You Didn't Take Out In The Rain

The Baldwin Chevelle is like a boy's toy from one of those plastic model kits that allow you to build the car in any of three styles: street, strip or show. The kid who built this one took everything from all three.

This car is not subtle or understated. It has electric windows and an electric rear window defroster. It has side-mounted exhaust pipes and ladder-type traction bars. Inside, the tach confronts you, hides the speedometer and leaves no doubt which kit it came from. Three shift levers jut out of the floor: a red-handled reverse gear lockout sneaks out of the back of the Hurst shifter boot, and a long lever on the passenger side, fitted like a four-wheel-drive transfer case lever, engages a mechanical overdrive. If one shifter is good, three must be "tougher."

At idle, the car is more speedboat. The twin burbling exhausts lack only the steam and froth alongside the hull to complete the image. With the doors closed and the windows zipped up, the trunk-mounted electric fuel

With 500 hp in a 3,900 lb coupe and a 4.88:1 final drive, it was difficult to start without leaving a mark, opposite. The power-weight-gearing combination made this kind of behavior possible in any gear. Motion Performance modifications were always performance oriented and little concern was given to graphic appearance. Still, the air induction hoods and side exhaust systems clearly suggested the nature of the Phase III cars, above.

pumps drone. They sound like ground auxiliary power units on a Boeing 727 while you're still at the terminal. These are high-capacity fuel pumps, and they push gallons forward, ready to do business.

Driving the car on the street is, in a word, scary. With the overdrive in high ratio (that is, 4:88.1 compared with 3:70.1), each gear is like low all over again. Once the car comes on the cam at 3500 rpm, it seems more to gather speed—albeit by cubic football fields—than to accelerate. Except for the tach skipping to 5000 rpm and the noise becoming a 140 decibel Bronx Cheer, you get no real sensation of speed increasing. But of course, you are simply melting your rear tires.

In each and every gear.

The abruptness with which things happen on the tach makes you wonder about the driver's coordination or perhaps motivation. The car behaves as though steady acceleration to 3500 rpm is followed by slapping of the pedal to the firewall. With each jump, the back

The large tachometer lashed onto the steering column was oriented to needle-at-the-top, time-to-shift, an important detail in a car where engine speeds leapt from 3000 to 5000 rpm in a heartbeat, opposite. Hurst's T-bar competition shifter was mated to a Muncie M–22 Rock Crusher four-speed, above. The small red lever at the rear of the shifter was a reverse-gear lockout. The Hone-A-Drive overdrive was engaged by pulling the black knob lever to the rear, shifting the final drive from 4.88:1 down to 3.70:1. The comfortable seats offered little side support but street racers rarely needed racetrack handling. Still, this Chevelle offered the cruising amenities of electric windows and rear window defogger.

The big flat Mr. Gasket air cleaner drew 780 cfm into the single Holley four-barrel carburetor. The Chevelle's LS-6 454 cast-iron block produced 500 hp at 6500 rpm and 500 lb-ft of torque at 4800. Sixties tire technology meant that the wildest muscle cars, skittish even on the driest concrete, went scurrying to safety at the first drops of rain. Late-night speed shops kept the lights burning and provided homes away from home, opposite.

Side-mounted exhausts, ladder traction bars, 454 engine, overdrive and electric windows—this car was not subtle or understated

end slips onto marbles and more rubber wears off. You drive by ear and eyeball. When the sound flattens out and peripheral vision returns, just grab another gear—it's time. At some point you run out of gears, reach down, arc the long overdrive lever back toward the seat and settle down to a nice cruise.

At 3000 rpm in fourth, in overdrive, you're making seventy miles every hour. The engine noise is still intrusive, but that's why you built this model the way you did. If you drove this car from New York City to Los Angeles, you'd arrive deaf. This is the car to drive to college if you live at home. You can work a part-time job that begins when the light turns green and ends twelve seconds later. You can earn your tuition on a Saturday night.

This is another of the Motion Performance built Chevrolets sold only through Baldwin Auto Company on Long Island, New

York. By 1969, Motion's owner, former drag racer Joel Rosen, was in his third year of collaborating with Baldwin on factory-warranted aftermarket-modified muscle cars. The company's own literature boasted that it was America's second-largest specialty performance vehicle producer, behind Shelby American. Born from a desire to offer customers a true street-strip performance car beyond what manufacturers would do, Baldwin Motion cars provided one greater benefit. They would be sold through an authorized Chevrolet dealer, which could also offer trade-in allowance, financing, insurance and delivery.

The size of Motion's operation allowed the firm extensive testing and development. Each car was run on a dynamometer before delivery. And the options list—most all of which was fitted to this particular Chevelle—was complete enough to quicken the pulse and shorten the elapsed time of any street racer.

At $4,998.88 plus the car, the full Phase III SS 454 Chevelle option replaced your stock 396 with an aluminum-head LS-6 454 ci engine. You got special cams, 12:1 compression requiring 103 octane fuel and Muncie's noisy-but-strong M-22 four-speed. You exchanged numerous factory pieces for Motion's Super-bite suspension, three-barrel Holley with aluminum manifold, Mallory ignition, twin fuel pumps, tuned headers and more.

A doctorate in street race came with each Baldwin Motion car. You earned the bachelor's degree first, to be a graceful winner, because you got so much practice at it. Your master's thesis dealt with the concept of hanging out; hard as it was to keep the Chevelle on the ground when the road was dry, you learned to hang out some place comfortable when it rained. The conclusion of your dissertation: You learned to never pass up a tire sale.

1970 Dodge Challenger T/A 340 Six-Pack

The Soulful Sound From Motown

Quick man, you gotta get down to the Dodge dealer. Order the Challenger JH23J and *don't* tell your folks. Take your trust fund, cash in those stocks. Who cares about college anyway. Go be a young Sam Posey, boy racer.

Heck! Sam Posey *is* young! So go be a younger Sam Posey. Read all those books about becoming a racing driver. Then, when you take the car home the first time, you'll learn the real definition of Dodge's Scat Pack. You'll hear your folks scream so long and loud you'll have to pack and scat!

So just what is this JH23J? It's the street version of Dodge's racer for the Sports Car Club of America Trans-Am series. Sam Posey's driving the real one. This year, though, the SCCA changed the rules and for 1970 all the entries have to be production based, meaning 2,500 or more get built.

But man-oh-man, what a boss set of wheels. It's the hottest machine this side of a racetrack fence. Just a word of advice, man. Don't go for some of those wild colors Dodge

Dodge introduced the Challenger for 1970 and included a Trans-Am production version. Built to qualify the racer in the production-based SCCA series, 2,700 were sold.

offers. None of this High Visibility Green or International Distress Orange. Think for a minute.

If, and it's a big if after this move, *if* your parents ever allow you back into the house, you may someday have to take Grandma—ah

yes, remember her, she of the trust fund fame—to Sunday tea. Right, you show up in some Post Nuclear Holocaust Green and see what she gets you next Christmas.

You got the picture yet? You tell your grandma it's a limited edition. You tell her, after all, last year Ford made almost 300,000 Mustangs and Dodge is only going to make a few of these. Tell her it's gonna be rare, like her dining room set.

Right, and get blue, Ice Blue Metallic. Subtle, man, classic blue. Right! Wedgwood blue, like her favorite china pattern. OK, OK, now you're thinking.

Oh, yeah, and this is important. Tell her it has a small V-8. Good for fuel economy. Hey cool your jets! This *is* a jet. This small V-8 is special, a hopped-up 340 like none other came before and it's topped with—you ready, man?— a Six-Pack. Yes sir, three Holley Deuces. Total combined cfm a mere 1150! Suck the doors off a Z-28 at a quarter mile. Right, yet when you drive her to tea, you're cruisin' on just the

center carb. So mileage is good, right. Fuel economy, pally, when you gonna catch on?

What about the mill? OK, it's no racer, but it's got good potential and Dodge already did some good things. The block has been stress relieved and they built extra iron into the main bearing area so you could use four-bolt mains (get your good buds at the speed shop to do it). The heads have been specially machined and the ports are offset—all the better to polish. The rods are longer and have these new ends that fit the adjusting screws in the new offset rocker arm . . . right, like the Hemi's. Tappets are high-rev hydraulics (yeah, so keep it below 6500, OK?), and best of all, those three Holleys sit on top of a new aluminum Edelbrock manifold. Altogether, 290 horses at five grand.

Have I made the point, yet? You *want* this car. The tranny? Oh, yeah, more good stuff. You can get the TorqueFlite, but tell Grandma the standard transmission is more economical. It's a new heavy-duty close-ratio four-speed, smoother than anything yet from Mopar. And it's got a Hurst pistol grip shifter. A little long in the throw, but hey, you can live with it, right? And a clutch you can live with, too. No more charley horse after a night of cruising.

And the suspension and tires really work. I know, you been riding with friends with 'Cudas and 'Stangs that slip off into the weeds.

Dodge stylists and product planners enjoyed themselves with the T/A and used hood scoops, pins, front air dams, blackout paint and decals. The T/A was a virtual rolling roaring test vehicle for rock and roll in motion. Dodge's 340 ci was fed by a trio of deuces, six carburetor barrels operated in progressive pairs, opposite. The intake sound through the large air scoop on the hood was joyous.

Hemis and Cobrajets are too heavy and they're built for the quarter anyway. This baby is made to go around corners, not through 'em. But you gotta get to a racer school, 'cuz Sam Posey says this car you can steer with your right foot. Just dive into a corner and play that gas pedal like the wah-wah pedal on my guitar and see what happens. Nose in, tail out. Just like dirt track racers. But you gotta be moving out because this thing runs E60s up front and G60 tires in the rear. Fat feet.

And wait till you see this machine. The product planning guys put enough bells and whistles on this to intimidate the weak and stun the brave—and outrage the War Department at home. Yeah, yeah, bucket seats, all the instruments, big tach and speedo right where they belong.

And the sound. Like listening to Jimi Hendrix at max on the dial. Twin side pipes. No, not like a Corvette's. These are trumpets! Fine sound. You know that tunnel near downtown? Take that some afternoon at about five grand. You'll blow out every window for blocks. They'll all think it's the big quake!

So here's what you do. You got money you haven't spent yet, so take about $4,100 and buy this car. Then go buy a book on race driving. And then go up on Mulholland and you show these funny foreign Porsches a thing or two about road cars. And when you've won a race or two, you call me and tell me how glad you are I made you buy this car.

OK, tell you what. If you don't like it, you keep it anyway, for your kid. Right, yeah, someday you'll have one—and you give it to him when he's smarter than you. And I guarantee you he'll love it. . . . Have *him* call me.

Quick man, you gotta get down to the Dodge dealer. Order the Challenger JH23J and don't tell your folks

The T/A exhaust pipes exited on the side of the car, ending just ahead of the rear wheels, above. The trumpet flares worked like megaphones, and the 290 hp, 340 ci small-block would snort and snap the T/A through the quarter-mile in 14.3 sec. at just under 100 mph. Different-size tires were used front and rear with white raised letters that helped set off the T/A styling of graphic stripes and lettering running along the car's sides, opposite. The optional rear window louvers complemented the rear spoiler and race-type filler.

1970 Dodge Coronet R/T 426 Hemi convertible

Coke-Bottle Voluptuousness

Dodge's stylists produced two masterpieces in 1970, with their Charger and its evolutionary Coke-bottle voluptuousness and with their long-hood, short-deck Challenger.

So where did the Coronet R/T come from?

If it were fair to suggest that Dodge's designers had reached the Renaissance with the Charger and Challenger, then the Coronet was the baroque.

Or, put it another way. If the Charger was James Bond and the Challenger was Peter Gunn, then the Coronet was Frank Mannix.

A television detective who slid down into this copper-colored baby would be grateful he'd always worn a shoulder holster. These seats were firm. Digging into his pockets, he'd fish past the Clorets to the ignition key. A quick twist into the ignition and the Hemi under the hood would warn any deviant behaviorist or disappearing two-timer or small neighborhood dog that he was on the move.

On the case.

Looking across the long hood, past the two functional air scoops, he'd compliment himself on his good taste. The color of this car was safe, better to tail the thieves, cheaters, philanderers and embezzlers that make up his life. Perhaps in another show, on another network, he might have given in to temptation, to investigate some of Dodge's catalog mysteries. For example, just what color was Go-Mango? Or Sub-Lime? But mysteries are a part of a TV detective's life.

Hemi Orange he knew. Every time he opened the hood, the elaborate plumbing of the Ramcharger system was there, in Hemi Orange. Might have been fun, in a Barracuda, he'd figure, but the copper color had class. Style. Power. Lots of power.

He'd lean forward, grabbing the Hurst shifter with its anatomical pistol grip. Would have reminded him of his snub-nosed revolver under his coat. He'd wiggle the lever into first, blip the gas once to give the neighbor kids a

thrill and ease out the smooth clutch. Being a guy who always took care of business, he'd congratulate himself on having ordered the Hemi engine with an option called The Read Out. All those gauges. Always impressed the babes. And he always knew he could never know too much about his equipment. No Show Boat option, no pink paint. Chrome wheels, bright colors. The suspect always spotted things like that.

He would have pulled out onto the boulevard and punched the gas. For all its weight, 3,600 pounds, it felt light. For its size, it felt

Dodge stylists changed the front end of the Coronet substantially for 1970 and created a few too many shapes, opposite. Only two Hemi R/T convertibles were sold. The other one was reportedly lost in a fire several years ago. Coronet base prices were low because many items were extra-cost options. By the time a buyer created a Hemi R/T such as this, the $3,800 base price approached $6,160. In retrospect, it's a bargain for such a rarity.

A complicated air induction system directed cold air off the hood into the giant Hemi air cleaner, opposite. Despite its 3,600 lb weight, the Hemi was sufficient to launch this opulent cruiser to 60 mph in 6.7 sec. and through the quarter-mile in 13.9 sec. at 105 mph. A most civilized muscle car, above, this rare Coronet was ordered with electric windows, a stereo cassette player and the Hurst pistol grip atop an almost corkscrew-like shift lever.

This was the last year Dodge produced a full-sized convertible. While its hood scoops functioned as part of a cold air system, the side intakes were strictly for show. The bumblebee stripe around the trunk recalled its Scat Pack heritage, opposite.

nimble. It was a big car. The 425 horses at his command could haul a Coronet up to sixty in less than seven seconds, and he knew 105 mph came in another seven after that. A quarter-mile at 105. All that and he'd still have wind through his hair. Never knew how these engines ended up in convertibles. Should have looked into that.

Amazing, only two Coronet Hemi convertibles were sold in 1970. And there were to be no more. Dodge had seen the clues. Hemis were offered in 1971, but the ragtop was finished in the Coronet line. Coronet would still have sedans and station wagons, great for undercover surveillance, but too far undercover for this star.

Maybe on another show on another network.

1970 Oldsmobile 4-4-2 W-30 455 convertible

If You Were Lucky, This Was Your Father's Olds

There was little unique about Oldsmobile's 4-4-2. It shared its platform with several other GM cars: Chevrolet's Chevelle, Buick's Gran Sport, Pontiac's GTO, each having grown off the 112 inch wheelbase. Of course, body panels differed. But engines, transmissions, suspension pieces and brakes were largely interchangeable. It made good business sense, good production sense, to design a car based on existing pieces or pieces that could be batch ordered to save costs.

Each division had a top-end entry: Pontiac's Judge and Buick's GSX competed for the buyer's attention against Oldsmobile's W-30 option. That made good marketing sense. Even if you'd never heard of a Hemi or a Super Cobrajet, plenty of variety was available from General Motors.

Olds' 4-4-2 (originally four-barrel carburetor, four-on-the-floor, dual exhausts) added the W-30 package in 1968, but sales performance lagged way behind the car's speed performance. By 1970, the mechanicals

were very similar to those in Buick's GSX. The 455 ci V-8 engine was rated at 365 hp, but with the W-30 Special Fit parts, its rating was 370 hp (identical to that of the GSX Stage I, and Pontiac's optional 455).

Exhaust emissions regulations had already begun to influence auto makers. Interestingly, this consideration eliminated the 400 ci engine (too dirty) from General Motors lines and brought out the 455. In Los Angeles, thorough air pollution researchers determined that if the vacuum advance line to the distributor was eliminated, it would substantially reduce exhaust emissions. This sacrificed performance in the name of clean air, but Oldsmobile had already seen the handwriting in the yellow skies.

The Oldsmobile's transmission-controlled spark system functioned from hydraulic pres-

Despite sharing platforms with the Chevrolet Chevelle, Buick GSX and Pontiac GTO, the Olds 4-4-2 W-30 version of the executive hot rod emphasized the hot rod.

128

The interior expressed the executive nature of the hot rod formula. A center console housed the Hurst Sport shifter. An Am-Fm stereo radio featured an 8 track cassette as well. Imitation burl wood surrounded three pods, which housed engine instruments, left, a speedometer, center, and large tachometer, right. Opposite, Olds' W-30 utilized two large hood-mounted cold air scoops to force-feed the Rochester four-barrel carburetor. Rated power from the 455 ci was 370 hp at 5200. Weight was reduced by using plastic wheelhouses, in bright red.

sure within the transmission and accomplished the clean air without losing the performance capability. Another Olds air quality control system sealed off the fuel system and replumbed any evaporated gasoline back through activated charcoal canisters. This prevented gas vapor from escaping into the atmosphere. Ahead of its time, and soon to be adopted by other GM divisions.

Olds approached styling somewhat differently. For a model close to the top of

General Motors' range, conservative treatment was expected. No matter. The two huge air scoops on the hood were plainly flamboyant. As part of the cold air induction system, however, they were not simply nonfunctional styling cues. They worked; indeed, the entire hood, of fiberglass with metal reinforcement, worked. What's more, front wheelwell liners were plastic, to further lessen weight over the front axle. And there was more: something like 50 pounds of acoustic insulation and sound-

The 4-4-2 originally designated four-barrel carburetor, four speeds on the floor and two exhaust pipes. Olds took performance seriously, eliminating nearly 100 lb of insulation and using some plastic panels instead of steel. This was the first year for W-30 cold air induction. Olds sold 264 convertibles, opposite. The 3,900 lb convertible W-30 was capable of 14 sec. quarter-mile times, at around 102 mph.

deadening material was removed to further lighten the car. And the intake manifold was aluminum, as was the quick-change differential housing.

Lightweight aluminum, quick-change differential . . . Something was going on here. Oldsmobile, ever in the vanguard of Union League clubs everywhere, witnessed new membership in the sons of traditional Olds buyers. These younger members had disposable income sufficient to want their cars a bit different from the rest, more suited to their own individuality, more personal cars. This may have been just another executive hot rod. But clearly the emphasis with the W-30 was more on the hot rod than on the executive.

1970 Pontiac GTO Judge 400 Ram Air IV convertible

Here Comes DeLorean!

Many enthusiasts believe that John DeLorean started all this with the Pontiac GTO. Perhaps; he was first to package a large engine in a small car for the public, give it a special name and concoct an entire marketing program around it. He found the right visionary people to help him, and mostly ignored those who didn't agree.

Pontiac Division came from death's door to breathe life into the entire GM giant before the sixties had ended. The man responsible was Bunkie Knudsen, who was appointed division general manager in 1956. Knudsen inherited an ailing car maker. His assignment meant restoring the division to profitability or going down in history as Pontiac's last general manager.

Knudsen discovered a line of cars known only for their dependability. No other image came to mind. His customers were older, fathers of the current generation. He knew this intuitively, but also as the result of mar-

By 1970, John DeLorean's lightweight muscle car had filled out some, and wore more make-up, opposite. A product of the rock and roll era, this GTO adopted the glitter of the most outrageous performers. It took its name from popular television. The well-equipped Judge was a hodgepodge of interior materials, above. Simulated wood met machine-turned metal and clashed with a fat race-style steering wheel. Full instrumentation included a clock and hood-mounted tachometer.

keting surveys, rare undertakings for a division. These surveys suggested that the postwar baby boom would bring a large population to car-buying age within a decade. Too late to help the 1957 or 1958 car lines, Knudsen set out to produce cars to appeal to this new young generation. Given freedom to do what he needed, he raided Oldsmobile and snared Elliott M. "Pete" Estes to be his chief engineer.

Knudsen and Estes found a young, unabashedly ambitious engineer for the assignment: John Zachary DeLorean, with Packard. Thirty-three, holder of twelve patents and countless other unpatented ideas, DeLorean admired the engineer in Henry Ford and the marketer-salesman in GM founder William Durant. He was made manager of Knudsen's newly created Advanced Engineering Department.

Knudsen took DeLorean under his wing from the start. DeLorean was introduced to all the passions of Knudsen's life, fine food, fine wine, fine art and auto racing. Knudsen took

his profits from an unexpected turn: as GM began urging six-cylinder engines on the other divisions, failing Pontiac was left with the dregs, the V-8s. Knudsen ignored GM's withdrawal from racing. He knew you could sell the boy's car to his father, but you couldn't sell the father's car to his boy. Racing appealed to the youth image Knudsen was courting.

Knudsen was already winning one significant race. In 1956, Pontiac sold 233,000 cars. In 1960, it sold 396,000, nipping at Chevrolet's heels. In 1962, Knudsen was named Chevrolet general manager; Estes took over as Pontiac's boss and DeLorean moved into Estes' former role as Pontiac chief engineer. A DeLorean follower, Bill Collins, was moved up into advanced engineering.

When DeLorean and Collins went to meet Estes for a preview of the second Tempest, quick-study Collins suggested lengthening the wheelbase to qualify for NASCAR. The three immediately wondered about larger engines. Over the weekend, DeLorean, fluent in foreign cars and grand touring, purloined a name. With a proper interior and suspension, the car would be a Grand Tourer. Building to legalize it for racing, to homologate it, DeLorean unhesitatingly stole the name of Ferrari's new sleek, stylish and extremely successful racer: GTO.

But it almost died in birth. Even as early as 1963, performance was getting a bad name. Accidents caused by drag racing were increasing. The corporate conservatives had grown shy. When Estes proposed the new GTO performance car, he was flatly refused.

Estes went ahead anyway, and made the GTO an inexpensive option within the LeMans line. A vote of no-confidence held initial production to 5,000 cars. Introduced in late 1963 for 1964, the GTO caught its skeptics off guard.

By year-end, nearly 32,000 GTOs were sold. DeLorean encouraged the bigger engines, but his most substantial contribution was stylistic, making the car look even wider, even meaner. By the end of 1965, the GTO was a line by itself.

Slowly, chief engineer DeLorean became salesman-marketer DeLorean. D'Arcy McManus advertising handled Pontiac's account. Account executive Jim Wangers, a racing enthusiast himself, had won a national drag racing title in 1960 in a Pontiac. Wangers watched the streets and knew the GTO had become a key element in a new culture of speed and freedom. DeLorean understood the message.

The culture had its own style of dress, speech and music. When the rock group Ronnie and the Daytonas sought to immortalize the GTO, DeLorean threw Wangers to the task, and the song sold more than 1 million copies. Other rockers had a more profound effect. With long hair and Creedence Clearwater Revival mustaches disappearing from pop music, the new look was wilder make-up, wilder clothes, wilder behavior. David Bowie and the Spiders of Mars strutted across the stage. Jethro Tull's showmanship, T. Rex's earrings and heavily rouged cheeks added a previously untried glitter and glamour to rock. The car stylists picked up on it. Flashy color splashes and strobelight interrupted graphics appeared where only bright color was dared before.

GTO sales topped 100,000. When the popular television show "Laugh-In" immortalized the line "Heah Come De Judge," Pontiac named its top-line GTO The Judge, fitted it with a rear air spoiler and gave it a wild paint job with multicolored splashes like eyeliner over the wheels. And John DeLorean, then a tender young forty, took over as general manager of a once-dead division.

The GTO was powered by the 400 ci Ram Air IV, opposite. The cold air force-fed engine was rated at 366 hp at 5100 rpm. By 1970, the manufacturers routinely underrated engine output to draw less attention from government and insurance industry watchdogs. Air conditioning and electric everything—seats, windows and door locks—were ordered, above. So was cruise control, tilt steering wheel and an Am-Fm 8 track stereo with sound booster. GTO Judge badges were everywhere. No longer a lean, mean muscle machine, the Judge needed 14.25 sec. for the quarter. With a car-load of options, the buyer paid $5,864 for this GTO Judge. Pontiac sold 168 Judge convertibles.

1970 Plymouth 'Cuda
426 Hemi Pink Panther
1971 Plymouth 'Cuda
426 Hemi

Powered By A Hemi, A Quarter-Mile At A Time

"That early Hemi engine was no great resounding success!"

In the cool light of history, Dave Long, a former development engineer on the Hemi engine, carefully reconsidered the hemispherical-head Mopar engine. The conclusion startled him. "The 426 was a production 'resurrection,' it was a wise solution to the marketing and product-planning guys who said they had to have a hot engine. But it was an old engine. The tooling was still around but by 1959, Hemis were replaced by the B engine, the 413. The Hemi was dead . . . and it was brought back from the dead."

Chrysler first used the hemispherical-head V-8 in 1951. In Chryslers and Imperials, it was a 331 ci engine that produced 180 hp. The DeSoto got a Hemi V-8 in 1952, a 276 ci block producing 160 hp. In 1953, Dodge joined the Hemi family with an engine having yet a third displacement: its 241 ci engine produced 140 hp. Then in 1955, a slightly overbored ver-

A munitions storage bunker's capacity was 12 rocket motors, 400 rocket igniters or 1,000 lb of explosives. One Hemi engined Barracuda coupe was a perfect fit, opposite. Approximately 736 Hemi 'Cuda coupes were produced in 1970. Of the 736 Hemi coupes sold, 411 went with three-speed TorqueFlite automatics. Base price was $3,160; this Pink Panther sold for $4,700.

sion of the 241 displaced 260 ci and was offered with either two- or four-barrel carburetors. The dual offered 167 hp; the quad

produced 177 hp. In a five-year span, Chrysler offered hemispherical-head engines in four different displacements as its corporate V-8s. It was Chrysler's first pushrod engine, the first overhead-valve engine, the first V-8 for Chrysler. And it was not without manufacturing and design problems.

"Problems with the first Hemis? Well . . ." Long recalls a number of drawbacks to using the first engines: "Very expensive, very complex, very heavy, very wide . . . with combustion roughness at idle. Benefits? Oh yeah, it was the most efficient combustion chamber design and it simply had one of the highest specific outputs of any engine design for the time."

Ironically, in 1956, when Plymouth got a V-8, it was not a Hemi but one of the first Wedges, a 303. Even with a 241 Hemi, the Plymouth could beat the big Chrysler 300 Letter Series cars because of the Plymouth's lighter weight; it was determined that the low-end Plymouth should not be demonstrably faster than the flagships. Not an easy equation to

solve. This Hemi head engine allowed the largest possible valves for its size. Yet valve stem angles meant the heads became quite wide. The heads projected far enough out from the centerline of the engine to make it difficult to assemble the car by dropping the body over the engine. So the heads had to be "squeezed" to accommodate production requirements: valve and pushrod angles were different for intake and exhaust sides. And the spark plug could go in only one place in the head, between the two valves, dropped deep down into the middle of all those valves, pushrods and rocker arms.

Despite the complications, the first Hemis grew in size, power and reputation. In 1955, the 331 produced 300 hp and a whole series of Chryslers were named for that output. In 1956, the 331 grew to 354 and output grew to 340 hp. Then in 1957, the 392 ci Hemi with 10:1 compression and a hot cam produced 390 hp. The Hemi engine remained in use through 1958 in Chrysler products.

Long reflects back: "That first Hemi outlived its usefulness very soon. We were smart enough to see that, to develop the A (318 ci) and B (383 and 413 ci) engines almost from the start. That first Hemi came into life as a solution to market needs for a V-8. But we simply didn't understand the problems at

Mopar marketing invented the Plymouth Rapid Transit System and included the Hemi 'Cuda as part of its high-performance commuter line-up. Wildly named colors were another marketing device. This is believed to be the only Pink Panther Barracuda remaining in existence. Ground-shaking power was the goal with Plymouth's Rapid Transit System, opposite. The dual Carter 550 cfm four-barrel carbs hid beneath a crackle-finish cold air induction hood. Hemis came from the factory with heavy-duty suspensions and a reinforced chassis.

first. And the problems put it under within a few years."

Tom Hoover joined Chrysler in 1955, with a master's degree in physics. After two years' further study at Chrysler Institute, his first project was the A311, development work on a 331 Hemi for Indianapolis. It never raced, but meanwhile, the 318 A engine was launched in 1956, and 413 B engines were installed into Imperials by 1959. These Wedge engines were simpler, less expensive. But over time, the Wedge proved to have one drawback. While it developed more torque at lower engine speed, it ran out of power at the top end. Put another way, the Wedge was a fine drag race engine, but the Hemi proved to be a better oval racing engine where speeds went up and stayed there. This is what brought the second Hemi into being.

"We had the drag scenario pretty much well in hand," Hoover remembers. "We had tuned manifolds, eight barrels. . . . But frontal area, drag coefficient . . ." Hoover stops, sounding like a contemporary engineer with concerns of the nineties. "The NASCAR situation was very different."

In 1961, Lynn Townsend was named Chrysler president. The NASCAR situation was a major concern of Townsend's.

"It was divine intervention, like a blessing," says Hoover, his excitement still fresh.

Likely one of the rarest Hemi 'Cudas, this coupe shows only 520 miles on the odometer, each one done a quarter-mile at a time, opposite. The original owner replaced the factory engine with a racing Hemi. Before its sale, the original engine was reinstalled. The orange-crate upholstery was an extra-cost option, on this page, a curious extra in a car purchased as a racer. The seats are not especially supportive but the cloth upholstery resists sliding—another inconsistency in a car meant for the straight line.

"Without Townsend's interest, it never would have gotten off the ground. Luckily he had a couple of teenage sons who were sensitive to the fact that the company's products were not attractive to their peers. The high output heritage of the company was related to working with Hemis."

Townsend put together a small group of engineers and designers with a goal of winning Daytona in 1964. "I walked into engine design," Hoover laughs, "with a 'change' slip. That sucker was signed by Lynn Townsend himself. Let me tell you that got action." With Townsend's signature, normal channels of operation were cleared away on every task. "Everybody was aboard. From kick off in April 1963, our target was the next February. We even had executive engineers down in the foundry doing the pouring." Then suddenly the A864 development cars were ready for testing.

Hoover was told to have car 702, a white 1962 model, out at the proving ground on a certain day. "It was just four of us. Townsend, his driver, me and car 702, out on the East-West straightaway. 'Tom, will these things beat the Pontiacs?' Townsend asked me. I said yes and he smiled. I ran it past him at full chat and he just smiled again, even bigger. He didn't even want to ride in it. He just wanted to hear it.

"I think it was a golden age. We won Daytona in 1964. What was so great of it was it wasn't stuff beyond the reach of the common man. Anyone could go to a store and buy it and use it.

"I'd do it again in a minute. Just let me get my toothbrush."

Long agrees, still amazed that going forward in 1963 meant stepping back to the fifties technology of the Hemi. "The new Hemi was done on a shoe string, because they

already had some tools," says Long. "It was the old Hemi tooling that we couldn't get rid of because nobody wanted it. It was scrapped tooling."

Some scrap! By this time, the 426 ci block had superseded the 413. Because Townsend's target was less than a year away, there was no time for a new engine. The engineers recalled the early Hemi's winning races in Chrysler 300s, so updating the old heads on the new block seemed most efficient. "It was strictly a marketing product planning thing," explains Long. "They asked what we could do to come up with a great engine."

The sun was quickly setting on American high performance, opposite. At the end of the 1971 model year, Chrysler withdrew its 440 Six-Pack, 426 Hemi and even its 383 engines from the model line. It was the last year when neck-snapping 5 sec. 0–60 times were available as a factory option. Horsepower ratings decreased as Chrysler adopted the net measurements. In fact, gross power was virtually unchanged even though compression was reduced slightly.

"The Hemi was strictly a marketing/product planning thing. They asked what we could do to come up with a great engine"

"Years before, we'd realized we could go nowhere with the Hemi on the street and we were smart enough to come up with a replacement. You could say we plucked the A and B engine out of a disaster. But then we recognized we could go no further with the Wedge on the racetrack and we were even smarter to come back with the Hemi. This time we resurrected a marketing legend out of [an] earlier success."

Long continues: "In terms of publicity it was a resounding success. And who can put a price on that."

Hoover agrees: "For the numbers produced it had impact beyond anyone's wildest imagination. I doubt if you're talking over four figures in production count. Think about the impact!"

But Long wraps it up: "What eventually killed the 426 . . . well in a way it really was never even born. It was just a thing we did for the marketing guys. The exhaust emissions would have cost too much to clean up. It finally died because of the dirty air."

1970 Plymouth 'Cuda 426 Hemi convertible
1970 Dodge Challenger R/T 426 Hemi convertible

Rise And Fall Of An American Dream

Outside Chrysler Corporation, Plymouth Division has been characterized as quick, intuitive and responsive, whereas Dodge Division has been slow, deductive and reactive. Where Plymouth saw the handwriting as it was spray painted onto the wall, Dodge waited until all the words were dry, then waited a bit longer to see how the lettering would age.

Plymouth got wind of a project spun off Ford's Falcon and responded quickly with its Barracuda spun off the Valiant. In fact, the response was so quick, Plymouth nearly beat Ford's Mustang to public introduction. Dodge

The first-generation Barracuda boasted the largest back window in production and didn't even offer a convertible. The styling evolution brought about a convertible and by this third edition, the 'Cuda had the American industry's smallest trunk. Completely restyled, the third-edition Barracuda in 1970 sat low, wide and aggressive, opposite. Only 14 were sold with Hemi engines in 1970.

watched it all, produced its Coronets, Chargers and Darts, and then watched some more.

Ford and Plymouth went through two body styles each and Chevrolet introduced its own entry before Dodge concluded that the handwriting was not fading. Performance compacts—muscle cars—might be a going thing.

So in late 1966, after Ford Motor Company had introduced its upscale Mercury Cougar, Dodge made the decision to jump into the market. Its target was the Cougar as its competition, and Dodge planned to make its new car, nameless at first, a "personal luxury car" to challenge Mercury for the same buyers that the Cougar attracted.

Dodge made good use of the delay in entering the market. While body designs were being proposed and rejected, a battle for power supremacy was raging furiously on the streets. In 1968 and 1969, Chrysler offered its Hemi in a wider range of models, competing with Ford, which had brought out its 428 Cobrajets, and Chevrolet, which had intro-

With 490 lb-ft of torque in a 3,800 lb package, the Hemi 'Cuda approached ocean-going tug proportions, above. Its $5,200 price on shore bought 13.5 sec. quarter-mile times, with 104.5 through the traps. It was called the Shaker because at idle, the entire engine vibrated visibly through the hole in the hood, opposite. It was claimed to be the largest air induction hood ever, protecting the two Carter 550 cfm four-barrel carbs hidden beneath it.

duced its 427s. So the product planners narrowed the trajectory even tighter and shot for the performance car market.

Thus, in 1970, when Plymouth and Dodge introduced new pony cars, both had done their homework. From a styling point of view, each car had advanced the requisite long-hood, short-rear-deck, low-roofline design to its furthest level of achievement. As if refining the styling of Ford and Chevrolet (both of whom were planning restyling out of this motif), Plymouth and Dodge produced low, wide, squat and aggressive-looking cars. They even further refined Pontiac's wide-track look as well.

At first glance, the cars seem to be identical twins, with only slight cosmetic differences between them. In fact, though they shared the same front and rear tire track, the new Challenger was 2 inches longer in wheelbase, nearly 4 inches longer overall, 1½ inches wider and a full inch lower than the Barracuda. The differences between the two were nothing compared with a principal difference they had from all the competition: they both offered high-performance convertibles, models out of production at Camaro and limited to small engines only in Mustangs.

Following its introduction in 1964, each successive edition of Plymouth's Barracuda shrank in overall length while the wheelbase remained constant. As a result, each new model separated the car further from its Valiant roots and the type adopted more clearly its own aggressive identity. The Barracuda's second fastback, from 1967 through 1969, was frequently characterized as a European Grand Touring design, and its advertising supported that image. Still Plymouth reminded American buyers that it was an American car with weather sealing that worked.

By 1970, as a part of Plymouth's marketing conglomerate called The Rapid Transit System, the division's thinking had changed so much that it no longer even manufactured a fastback; having started life with the largest back window ever in an automobile, the latest Barracuda flip-flopped proportions and boasted the smallest trunk ever in an automobile, not quite 6 cubic feet. The new car was 6 inches shorter, 2 inches lower and 5 inches wider than the former European Grand Touring aspirant. Instead, American street slang became the style dictator, and the 'Cuda was born as the ultimate performance Rapid Transit ride.

The Challenger entered the market with the most complete line and widest variety of

If you couldn't find the car you sought from Plymouth's Rapid Transit Barracuda or Dodge's Scat Pack Challenger line, it would only be because you needed four doors

any muscle car in history. There was no trial and error, no lag time, nothing tentative about it. Unlike with other introductions, all the options were there the first year, everything, up to flat-out quarter-mile speed, was right from the moment the showroom doors opened.

Once the decision was made to go ahead, the engine driving the project must have been a Hemi, because it got there right away.

Ordering a Barracuda or a Challenger in 1970 was not a task for the indecisive. Nine engines were available in either car. There was a choice of eighteen colors on either car. Three levels of each model were offered, each in coupes or convertibles, all available with outrageous graphics and spoilers, and leather, vinyl or cloth seats. There was even a choice of hood air scoops. Oh, to order the Shaker hood

The interior's space age styling was accomplished with molded plastic panels. Instrumentation was complete with speedometer and tachometer, above. Opposite, the Hemi convertible was an intriguing blend of raw muscle car and stylish cabriolet.

151

By 1970, many American GIs had returned from Viet Nam with combat pay in their pockets and an unsatisfied hunger for America's muscle. Dodge introduced its Challenger, and offered a convertible with its Hemi engine. Nine were sold. Parked on the flight deck at Channel Islands Air National Guard base, this Challenger, painted Plum Crazy, was ready for takeoff, opposite. The Hemis started easily and a full-power run-up was well within design parameters.

Automatic transmissions with low-stall-speed torque converters meant each shift from neutral chirped the tires. A heavy foot produced much more than a chirp. The 426 Hemi R/T convertibles turned sub 6 sec. 0–60 mph times and finished the quarter just a tick over 14. Above, the great IQECAG: A military acronym? Incredible Quivering Exposed Cold Air Grabber. There are many who would describe a C–130 in the same terms. Opposite, night ground crew duty or part of the flight manifest? Strapped to a pallet, the Hemi Challenger was smaller and lighter than a tank and certainly much faster. Only seven of these convertibles are known to exist.

or Air Grabber without a Hemi engine but with a 440 four-barrel? Or not? Oh, decisions, decisions. Or not at all! Each car was also offered as a simple, plain, economy compact commuter.

If you couldn't find the automobile you sought from Plymouth's Rapid Transit Barracuda or Dodge's Scat Pack Challenger line, it would only be because you needed four doors.

And just when you had thought it out, taken time to sort through the abundance, summoned up the courage and sharpened up a box of pencils, both makers introduced their Trans-Am race series cars. Plymouth brought out a street version of its All American Racers 'Cuda, run in the SCCA series by Swede Savage and Dan Gurney, while Dodge introduced its T/A, as raced by Sam Posey.

The Trans-Am spin-offs lasted only one model year. Plymouth and Dodge decided not to participate in the series in 1971. But the

handwriting on the wall was reading differently than it had four years earlier. Late in the summer of 1970, near the end of the model year, when only 151 big-engine Challenger and 'Cuda convertibles had been sold, Chrysler understood what Ford had done. Dodge's Challenger convertible was removed from the line-up; it had been a one-year wonder. The end of the next year saw the end of the 'Cuda convertible and the deletion of the Hemi from all options. Another two years would see the end of both cars, after barely a decade for the Barracuda, a mere four years for the Challenger.

Their run had been remarkable. Their fully optioned introductions had left no possibilities unavailable. But quick, intuitive Plymouth and slow, deductive Dodge had left one option unconsidered: for the first time in history, someone offered Too Much, Too Late.

1971 Dodge Challenger R/T 426 Hemi

Calling GM And Ford's Bluff

In 1971, Barry Newman starred in the film *Vanishing Point.* Playing a man with no first name, simply called Kowalski, he actually costarred. Because as the loyal fans who have watched it over and over would tell you, the real star was a Dodge Challenger coupe.

After swallowing a handful of amphetamines, Kowalski bets his speed merchant that he can leave Denver and be in San Francisco fifteen hours later. High on speed, Kowalski disappears into the late night, and soon the film does too. In the next 100 minutes, the lessons of life in the fast lane are mixed with better living through chemistry. During some of the film's longer moments, Kowalski becomes a modern cowboy folk hero, in an existential battle against the establishment just for the sake of going up against it.

For car buffs, some of the film's more successful moments involve that Challenger, some masterful stunt driving and some enjoyable sound recording.

Dodge Division has probably never determined whether starring in motion pictures had the same effect on buyers as winning races was supposed to have had. It is likely that a few rugged individuals hurried on down to their local Mopar dealers and got their own speed fixes.

The 1971 Dodge Challenger Hemi differed mostly in cosmetics from the 1970 introductory models. The grille and rear end were busied up, and nonfunctional scoops were added ahead of the rear wheels. The Hemi's Shaker hood was eliminated, replaced with two functional slash scoops. Inside, door panels adopted the simulated wood motif on the

The Challenger, opposite, last of The Scat Pack high-performance group from Dodge, was advertised apologetically: "It ain't Attila the Hun but it ain't Mild Mary either." Attila's days were numbered. The hood scoop slashes, on this page, resembled sculptured high relief surfaces seen from above. The clean, open grille from 1970 was busied up for 1971. Hood pins disappeared.

Dodge's 1971 Challenger approached a stylistic vanishing point, opposite. Super graphics were gone. Shaker hoods were gone. Still used were the racing-style gas filler caps, and raised lettering on the hood still announced engine size. Two functional slash hood scoops fed outside air into the Hemi, on this page. Horsepower, rated at 350 net, was a figure taken at the rear wheels. Gross rating was still 425 but insurance companies had begun invoking a 25 to 50 percent surcharge on high-horsepower cars. In all, only 71 R/T Hemi coupes were produced. Of these, 59 had four-speed transmissions, while only 12 were built with automatics.

High performance had reached a vanishing point. Muscle cars, it seems, were destined to go out with a whimper

dash, and the stitching changed direction on the seats.

Beginning in 1971, throughout the entire American automobile industry, pressure came down for more accurate and responsible horsepower figures. The manufacturers were told to take readings at the rear wheels—through all the drivetrain gears—rather than off the flywheel. Numbers reflected net brake horsepower rather than the higher gross figures.

What's more, the Environmental Protection Agency decreed that a certain percentage of each manufacturer's fleet must operate on lower-lead-content gasoline. Compression ratios came down on medium and smaller engines, though for 1971, this didn't affect Chrysler's Hemis or 440s.

Dodge Division, and everyone else for that matter, took notice. New, strict engine emissions standards and safety equipment requirements were being proposed everyday in Congress. Insurance companies, now aware that only sports drove sports cars and that high horsepower meant high performance, which meant higher risk, responded with higher rates. A Hemi was an expensive liability—to an insurance company and an enthusiast owner alike.

With 1971 Hemi R/T coupe sales amounting to just less than one quarter of 1970's 287 sales, Dodge pulled the plug on not only the Hemi but the 440s and even the 383 engines in Challengers for 1972. The Scat Pack, born in 1968, was being picked off one by one. Some of the Challenger advertising in 1971 featured an R/T coupe, announcing, "It ain't Attila the Hun, but it ain't Mild Mary either." The text still invited enthusiasts to see their dealers if they were interested in the Hemi or 440 engines.

But in 1972, the ads told you, "Good looks can get you anywhere." And the brochure reasoned: "The way things are today, maybe what you need is not the world's hottest car [but a car that is] reasonable to buy, to run. About as enjoyable in the legal range as anything its size. And a lot more thoughtfully done."

Mild Mary had arrived, following legislators, emissions controllers and insurance underwriters in the door. High performance had reached its own vanishing point. Kowalski challenged a narrow opening in the legal system and went out with a bang. Muscle cars, it seems, were destined to go out with a whimper.

1971 Dodge Charger R/T 426 Hemi

Known By The Company You Keep

You give a quick glance as you pass the mirror. Shoot your monogrammed Troy Gill shirt cuffs. "Show 'em just a flash of the Cartier Tank watch," you warn yourself. Your Polo suit and your perfect Gucci ribbon "bit" loafers shimmer back at you in the mirror installed behind your washroom door.

"Hmmm! They don't even know what an investment loophole is and yet I'm inventing 'em. Burying money for people who don't even know they need it buried yet." Snatch your camel's hair British Warmer off the hanger and sail past your foxy new secretary, a perk from your promotion.

"Meeting at the pier, Miss Dawes, won't be back." Miss Dawes gazes up admiringly, catch-

The front air dam was optional, so was the vinyl roof, opposite. Completely restyled for 1971, the third-edition Charger epitomized Chrysler's attempts at a Coke-bottle silhouette. Three inches shorter than in 1970, the car still looked bigger and heavier.

ing a glimpse of your freshly razor cut hair. "Yes, sir. Good luck, sir!" she says. Her desire hangs in the air like a veil, her eyes sparking like flares in the fog.

Luck! Luck! You frown to yourself. Luck is for losers. You don't need luck. It's 1971, you've just been annointed Best and Brightest, youngest VP the firm has ever had. Perks have been thrown at you. You're a Captain of Industry. You develop money-losing investments that don't really lose money! You create ways to not lose money and still write off investments. You are *the* creative genius in creative loss in the city. You provide people with benefits they don't yet even know they need.

Step out into the cool winter day. Your Warmer hangs, perfectly tossed over your shoulder.

"Hey, G.C. What you driving these days?" your buddy T.R. asked you at the handball club the other morning.

Another perk, you remind yourself. First one of the bright boys to get a company car!

What else? you snort to yourself, but put on an air of sublime boredom. "Charger R/T Hemi." The word Hemi comes out overemphasized, despite yourself. You vow to practice how it will just fall off your tongue the next time someone asks.

"Hemi, G.C.? Man you must've created some tough loopholes the last few months. The insurance must kill you."

You crouch to serve, call "ready" and wonder why this other supposedly brilliant Harvard-via-Choate MBA is asking you about insurance. Oh, really.

"Company car, T.R. Coulda had anything. Jag, Corvette, anything. I chose it, they bought it. They maintain it. They insure it. I drive it." With that you smashed a final service ace into the deepest, darkest corner. It died with a pop and dribbled back toward T.R.'s feet. You took him two games, gave him one. Always. "You know, T.R., you'd really enjoy this game more if you took a few brush-up lessons. Maybe we oughta skip next week. . . ."

Humming along now, the coast road is clear. Midday the traffic is always open for a Captain of Industry. When will they raise these speed limits to something realistic, you wonder. The Hemi burbles along at eighty, ten over the limit. At this speed, another all-too-short five minutes and you're there. Papers in your thin Mark Cross briefcase, ready to be signed, and three new clients think you're a genius

Optional Hemi power moved the 4,000 lb Charger from 0 to 60 in 6 sec. flat, left. The standard R/T engine was the 440 Six-Pack, half a second slower to 60. A Ramcharger cold air induction system came with the Hemi. The top-of-the-line Charger sold for $4,600. Opposite, bucket seats were made optional in 1971, in order to reduce prices. But with electric windows and a cassette stereo with record feature (for the executive on the go), few options were missed on this example.

With all the possibilities available on a Chrysler Corporation order form, including as many as nine engines in some models and more than 20 colors, it was easy to specify equipment and create a unique personal luxury muscle car. Opposite, black paint mirroring the sunset, this black-on-black-on-black Charger is among the heaviest optioned and the only one built in this color scheme. Only 63 Hemi Chargers were sold, 33 with automatics, as this was.

When they ask, Hey, what are you driving these days? you snort and say, What else? Charger R/T Hemi

again. A guru, they called you, an investment guru!

Some loser pulls onto the freeway in front of you. Your exit is just ahead to the right. Some guy in one of those imports, crawling.

"Pedal faster," you sneer to yourself, and decide your expression is unattractive as you notice yourself in the rearview. But the car does the real menacing. You reach down, find and yank the Ramcharger Air Grabber hood scoop with the aggressive instincts of a street fighter crouching before the uppercut. Your Charger bellows and sucks the doors right off the offending intruder. The other car swerves measurably as you explode past, dragged into your wake. After all, this is 1971, the start of a new decade of Hemi power!

You pull up in front of the pier. Out there, oil pumps are going up and down, and here, you're with three big-dough clients with imagination and too much tax obligation. "Park right on the pier," you tell yourself. Because no one else has dared.

The air is crisp. Pelicans dive and cry and swirl around the pier. As you idle out, sea gulls take flight one by one when you rumble past. Their flight marks your progress. At the second wide spot, you park.

A worktable has been set up. You slip the crude-oil-black Mark Cross case up, and pull out your clients' papers and your Mont Blanc. They stand around awaiting their turns at signing away money they have for loopholes they will need.

"By the way, you know this makes you all very visionary. Investing in oil exploration will be the next big thing. Costs are high, risk is great, write-off is impeccable. And right now with plenty of cheap oil . . ." And you assume your own signature: your jacket still buttoned, your hands slip through those high side vents and into your pockets. People know you by what they see.

"By the way, G.C.," one of them says, pausing after his middle initial, "great car. Hemi, isn't it?"

1971 Dodge Charger Super Bee 426 Hemi

Merged Into Oblivion

As Chrysler Corporation stepped into the seventies, the Environmental Protection Agency took its first steps at strangulation. In 1971, Dodge Division installed a vapor saver at government direction. This device limited gas tank evaporation. By 1972, the beginning of the end of muscle cars was on the horizon.

Engines were redesigned to meet exhaust emissions standards instead of performance goals. Nearly all Chrysler engines ran on unleaded gas because compression ratios were lowered. Horsepower figures were reduced. To curry favor with the insurance companies, the corporation began quoting net horsepower figures at the wheels instead of gross readings from the flywheel. Even the Sure-Grip limited-slip differential, while still offered, was listed

Only 22 Hemi Super Bees were sold in 1971, opposite; 13 had automatics. Most of the options on this $4,600 coupe were under the hood and outside: front dam, rear wing, vinyl roof and the Hemi engine added most to its $4,000 base price.

as a safety feature, not a performance option.

In 1970, sales slacked in Dodge's intermediates, the Chargers and Coronets. The cause stemmed from the duplication of body styles and options in the two models. Dodge had tried to offer a full range of body styles from each of its model lines, and at one point there were said to be 200 lines one could check on a Dodge order form. Production lines were tied up building virtually identical cars with different model names. Unwittingly, this was to benefit future collectors: with all the combinations of color, engine, transmission and body style, it is understandable how only one copy of a given car could be built.

So Dodge product planners reconfigured the Coronets and Dodge stylists redesigned the Chargers. Coronets were to be four-door automobiles only. Chargers would be two-doors only, and there would be no convertibles. The Super Bee, which had been a Coronet equivalent to Plymouth's Road Runner, would slide over to the Charger column.

Restyled now, the Charger shrank in wheelbase by 2 inches, in overall length by 3 inches and in rear overhang by 4 inches. But the car grew in width by 2½ inches and in front overhang by 3 inches. Subtly, it appeared even larger.

Differences between the two cars at the top of the line were slight. The Charger R/T sported R/T medallions and featured two long scallop-shaped nonfunctional vents on each door. The Ramcharger Air Grabber hood scoop was introduced to the Charger line for 1971 and was standard on the R/T but optional on the Super Bee.

The standard engine on the Super Bee was the 383 ci Magnum V-8 with a four-barrel carburetor producing 300 hp and coupled to a three-speed on the floor. The 440 Six-Pack and Hemi engines, a four-speed and an automatic were available as options. The standard power for the R/T was the 440 Magnum (370 hp gross) with the TorqueFlite automatic on the column. The 440 Six-Pack (385 hp gross) and

The only concession to graphics was a hood bulge and this optional Ramcharger cold air induction hood scoop, on this page. It was activated by a switch under the dash. Closed, it fit flush against the hood. It was available in 1971 only. The heart of the matter, opposite. A completely original Hemi with its dual Carter four-barrel carburetors. For 1971, federal safety and emissions standards required horsepower ratings be measured at the rear wheels. While the engine still rated 425 gross, it advertised 350 net.

2001

Its family resemblance is obvious, opposite. The Super Bee became part of the Charger line-up for 1971, as the model just beneath the R/T. Originally a Coronet model, the Super Bee was Dodge's answer to Plymouth's Road Runner. Few options were ordered on this Super Bee, above. A Tuff Formula Racing steering wheel was optional, as was the column-shift TorqueFlite. Bench seats were standard. The Ramcharger Air Grabber scoop and manual chokes operated from below the dash.

Hemi (425 hp gross) were still optional.

One new item on the option list came about as a direct result of the Pontiac GTO Judge. Front and rear spoilers were offered for both the Super Bee and Charger R/T, though according to several sources, they were an option checked by few buyers.

Fuel economy, still of little concern in the days of gallons for less than 35 cents each, was around 10 mpg for a Super Bee equipped with a 440 Six-Pack, and around 11 mpg for a Hemi in an R/T or Bee.

The 1971 model year was the last in which performance was a selling point. Dodge's marketing thrust for 1972 stressed comfort and luxury in the Charger line. Federal safety requirements and exhaust emissions controls increased. And the 440 Six-Pack and the Hemi engine were never offered again.

1971 Plymouth Road Runner 426 Hemi

Chrysler's Hemi Corvette

The Plymouth Road Runner was a purpose-built automobile. The approach was purely methodical, as coldly calculated as any racing manufacturing effort. The championship at stake here was for the customer's dollar. Every effort was made to win. And win it did.

For a while.

In the end, much as with racing rule making, the sanctioning bodies for the public roads so restricted the winner that it lost. It limped on in the marketplace. When it finally with-

Plymouth advertising referred to its rounded shapes for 1971 as fuselage styling, opposite. The body appeared more shaped by the wind than had past folded-paper, hard-edge styles. The Road Runner was an entry-level full-size Plymouth. The Hemi logo, the flat-black hood power bulge and hood pins announced the power and suggested the intention of the Road Runner, on this page. One of 55 built with a Hemi, it would just break 14 sec. in the quarter-mile at 103.5 mph.

drew from the contest, it was the customer who had lost the most.

One day in the winter of 1967, the phone rang in Joe Sturm's office. Sturm was one of Plymouth's product planners, having started his life with Chrysler as an engineer. The sales division was calling, asking him if Plymouth should create a new car with "the biggest engine we make as standard equipment. A car with no back seat, floor mat. . . . Eliminate every piece of trim and ornamentation?" A two-seater? Hemi? Certainly a race car. A Plymouth Corvette?

Sturm bounced the idea up and down the hall, concluding it was good but had a limited market. But with some modification . . .

The Mustang was already three years old, and with Chevy's new Camaro just out, a new hole existed for a car with every attention to powertrain, chassis and brakes, and little attention to tinsel and chrome. A thorough marketing survey done for the GTX pointed out a street-racer-cruiser market that was not

yet satisfied by Ford's and Chevrolet's models.

Sturm and his staff analyzed the competition, with particular attention to performance and acceleration. Their conclusion was no surprise to racers: the more you spent, the faster you went. A significant target appeared. The marketing staff recognized that to do at least 100 mph in the quarter, you had to do at least $3,300 in the showroom. They set out to produce a car that would give that performance for $3,000, delivered.

Plymouth stripped interiors to bare bones, reserving the bulk of the customer's dollar for mechanicals. A 383 V–8 was modified: heads, cams, manifolds and other parts came from the 440. The free-breathing engine produced 335 hp and initially was unique to the new car. Plymouth offered the Hemi too, for an extra $700. Four-speed gearboxes were standard, but the TorqueFlite was optional. Suspension was heavy-duty, perfected from experience on the drag strips. Disc brakes were optional. Bucket seats consumed too much of the budget, so a bench was standard.

Product planning had a list of names for the car, one of which had been around for quite some time but suddenly seemed appro-

The Road Runner was conceived as purposefully as any road racer. Introduced in 1968, it would do 100 mph in the quarter-mile and sell for less than $3,000. Between creature comforts and government controls, the price for the same performance in 1971 was $4,850. The complicated vacuum-operated Air Grabber cold air induction scoop hangs from the underside of the hood, opposite. The massive air cleaner fitted flush with the rubber sealer at the base of the Air Grabber and the Hemi engine lurked below.

priate. Sturm was told to stay home Saturday morning and watch television.

Permission came from Warner Bros. to use the name and the copyrighted character of the Road Runner. When Plymouth's outside manufacturer used copper instead of aluminum wire in the horns, the Road Runner's "Beep-beep" identity on the road virtually matched the cartoon character's on the screen.

Just like the cartoon character, Plymouth's car was quick. Through the traps, the new Road Runner ran 98 mph, a mere 2 mph below the target. But the two-door coupe was to sell for $2,900, beating that target by a comfortable margin. A hardtop at $3,000 and a convertible for $3,300 were also part of the line-up.

At the last minute, the marketing and sales staffs got cold feet, predicting no more than 2,500 Road Runners would be sold. When 45,000 went out of showrooms in 1968, excitement and joy mingled with sheer astonishment.

In 1969, the options list grew by leaps and bounds. Bucket seats could be had. The Air Grabber cold air induction scoop was offered. And the little black horn under the hood was painted purple and labeled Voice of the Road Runner to give the folks a thrill when they asked to see it.

Motor Trend named the Road Runner Car of the Year in 1969, and Plymouth responded by introducing a 440 Six-Pack. The hood, painted flat-black, was fiberglass and was held in place by four chrome pins just as on Plymouth's Super Stock Hemi racers. With the 440, quarter-mile trap speed was up to nearly 110 mph. And in 1969, Plymouth sold 85,000 Road Runners.

Plymouth poked some fun at Washington

A clean dashboard was arranged with legible instruments logically placed in the Road Runner, above. An Am-Fm radio as well as the Tuff steering wheel were optional, as were bucket seats. Only 28 of the Hemi Road Runners used four-speed transmissions with Hurst pistol grip shifters. Cold air induction was no longer legal in California by 1971, right. Called an unsilenced air cleaner, the state's laws regulated not only safety and air quality but also noise. It was the eleventh hour for American high-performance cars, opposite. Chrysler's last hurrahs were these Hemi engined muscle cars, which still had less than 10 lb of weight per horsepower.

The effect of insurance surcharges meant that even safe drivers could have insurance payments equal to their car payments. Warning lights were flashing throughout the auto industry

lobbyists in 1970 when it introduced its Rapid Transit System product line. The body of the Road Runner was softened slightly, a redesign freshening up its looks. The lightweight fiberglass hood for the 440 Six-Pack was replaced by the Air Grabber. More interior options appeared to dress up the original Spartan speedster. One outside graphics option ran half the length of the car, showing the Road Runner with a long trail of swirling dust.

It was not only Washington that couldn't take a joke in those days. The insurance industry, aware that high performance from Detroit put it at high risk, began to initiate surcharges. For cars with fewer than 11 pounds per horsepower, surcharges ranged from twenty-five to fifty percent! And sales of Road Runners dropped by about fifty percent.

For 1971, the Road Runner was completely restyled, assuming Plymouth's fuselage shape. The rounded body became more masculinely aggressive, with swelled fender flares. Both the coupe and convertible were dropped

from production. Exhaust emissions requirements were beginning to be felt. The 383, still the stock engine, rated 300 hp as compression was reduced to make it run on lower-octane gas. Sales brochures for the first time published gross and net horsepower figures, listing the optional 440 as 385 and 330 hp. Even the venerable Hemi suffered indignity: its compression was reduced a notch. Though its gross power was still 425 hp, its listed net output was 350 hp.

Options again increased, including wilder graphics and a rear spoiler. But sales declined drastically. The effects of insurance surcharges meant that even safe drivers could have insurance payments equal to their car payments. Plymouth sold barely 14,484 Road Runners. Warning lights were flashing throughout the auto industry.

By the 1972 model year, the Hemi was dead. Plymouth's brochure, which had listed both gross and net horsepower figures in 1971, listed no power ratings in 1972.

1971 Plymouth 'Cuda
426 Hemi convertible

The Greatest Story Ever Told

No one would deny that cars have personalities. Some are finicky, contrary, mean-spirited and high-strung; some are high-spirited, lovers of the run, better the faster they go; others are mellow, compliant, quick to warm to the task and willing partners, without balkiness. And we give them names, like pets, names that stick for all their lives with us.

Of course, they're only machines. Still, we look at them, in parking lots or used car lots, or in museum collections, and wonder what their names are, what their lives have been.

Cars in collections interest us especially. They may have belonged to some celebrity at some time or other. In the Vintage collection are classic cars, a Duesenberg that belonged to actor Joe E. Brown, and a Packard, the Car of the Dome, built for the 1936 New York World's Fair. There is a Porsche 917, a race car from the same era as these muscle cars. It ran at Le Mans and on nearly every lap for twenty-four hours touched 240 mph along the Mulsanne

Styling changed slightly from 1970 to 1971, opposite. The front end became compartmentalized, with quad headlights and sectioned egg-crate grille. In 1971, 108 Hemi 'Cudas were built, only seven of which were convertibles. In a concession to increasing insurance and safety concerns, Plymouth sales brochures quoted both 425 gross hp and 350 net hp.

straight. This same 917 ran in the movie *Le Mans*, driven by Steve McQueen. The stories these cars could tell. Oh, if only they could talk.

By 1971, the Hemi engine was near the end of a second life. The first Hemi was on a scrap heap by 1959. But Chrysler answered its racers' needs and resurrected the tooling. What was born again was a whole new generation of cars of the dome-head. What would they say about resurrection?

The first Hemis could talk of ruling the roads, of massive comfortable cars rolling almost silently along the new American interstates. Wide, smooth Chryslers effortlessly consuming miles of wide, smooth roads. Those cars, probably called Edmund or Beatrice, Victor or Rowena, likely never met cars called Cruiser 14 or Car 6 or Unit 10. Hemi-powered Dodge police cars would have had few conversations with a Rowena or an Edmund.

No, Unit 10 would have known of Traveller, a car named for the horse of Confederate general Robert E. Lee. Traveller was a Chrysler 300D owned by a man called Jerry Rushing. Traveller's modified 392 Hemi could tell tales of running away from Cruiser 14 or Car 6.

The sixties had been the decade of space exploration, opposite. The new decade's 'Cudas used molded one-piece plastic door panels and molded dash and console to achieve space age styling. Above, despite federal safety concerns, emissions standards and insurance industry attention, the Hemi 'Cuda was still a performer. With 425 hp for 3,980 lb, this last muscle car was good for sub 6 sec. 0–60 runs all day long.

Insurance surcharges, emissions controls, safety concerns and gasoline up to 38 cents a gallon: for the second time in its life, the Hemi was dead

Traveller ran liquor, as fast as 140 mph, it is said. Traveller would laugh because he was never caught. And when television began to imitate life, the Dukes of Hazzard renamed Traveller the General Lee. Oh, the stories those flying Chargers could tell, the things they'd know....

The latter-day Hemis raced at first. High-speed runs with hours of turning left. What tricks did the Junior Johnsons perform beneath their hoods? They'd never tell. Then the racing rule makers required thousands of us to own Hemis for a few of us to race them. Cars of the dome-head came to the streets for the second time.

They raced too. Battles under the streetlights. These cars had names: Charger, Road Runner, Super Bee, GTX, Superbird, Challenger, Barracuda! Aggressive names, evocative of their purpose. To hunt, to race, to win, to not tell stories away from home.

Most of these cars were coupes. Closed cars, cars where the driving experience at speed was more like that in a modern video arcade surround-sound game. And after the race, what else went on? Who's to tell?

But the convertibles, the open cars, cars built to a different purpose . . . Surely there must be some stories to tell.

Throughout the 426 Hemi era, roughly 10,000 engines were installed in road cars; some records claim fewer than 6,500. During this same five-year period, Chrysler Corporation produced nearly 8,420,000 cars. But only 179 Hemi convertibles were known built; one car in every 47,000. This is not mere exclusivity here, we're talking nobility, maybe royalty.

And of course, royalty never talks. By the time you get near the end of the royal family line, the blood line thins. In 1970, twenty-seven Hemi convertibles were born. The stories they would tell were of increasing difficulty breathing, increasing cost of insuring their lives, increasing restraints by safety-conscious nannies. The joyful, youthful years of their fathers, when gasoline was plentiful and cheap at 19 and 22 cents a gallon . . .

But the cars didn't talk. The conversations in those days were held around desks

and tables in the meeting rooms and offices at Lynch Road and Hamtramck and in the Six Story Building, as Chrysler headquarters was known.

In the last year, the convertible line was dropped from the Challengers, Coronets and Road Runners. Only the Barracuda remained. Chrysler's open cars of the dome were the last of the breed, royal offspring given names such as True Blue, Sno White, Formal Black, Tor-Red, In-Violet, Sassy Grass Green . . . or Lemon Twist Yellow.

On May 19, 1971, the last of the dynasty was born. Outside, insurance underwriters spoke of careless tendencies of muscle car drivers and premiums in the Midwest went up to $550 per year for a Hemi 'Cuda, $800 if you lived in a major city, and those rates applied only if your record spoke of no mistakes.

By mid-May, late in the model year, Plymouth had built only seven Barracuda convertibles with the Hemi. Production would continue through the end of the model year. Another Hemi coupe or two would be built. Retooling for the 1972 model year was to begin shortly. Outside, OPEC talked about the future of crude oil. Gasoline was up to 38 cents in Los Angeles. Conversations going on in Chrysler's headquarters dealt with mistakes of the future. The open car would be one. The dome-head engine would be another.

Future mistakes, they agreed, should be limited to the unforeseeable. There was no more talk. For the second time in its life, the Hemi was dead.

Three body styles, nine engines, 18 colors, 75 options. Advertising reminded buyers that Plymouth came through for them to produce the muscle car they wanted, opposite. Manufactured on May 19, 1971, this is known to be the last Hemi engined convertible Chrysler ever produced, above.

Specifications

1964 Dodge Ramcharger Superstock 426 Hemi Cross Ram

The only acid-dipped steel-body sedan factory lightweight Hemi Ramcharger Superstock known to exist. First year of 426 ci Hemi engine.

Engine: Chrysler 426-R Hemi
      426 ci from 4.25 in. x 3.75 in.
      425 hp @ 6000 rpm
      480 lb-ft @ 4000 rpm
      12.5:1 compression
      Dual Carter 4V carburetors and Cross Ram aluminum air intake

Transmission: Four-speed manual with Sure-Grip limited-slip and 3.55:1 final

Chassis: Wheelbase: 119.0 in.
      Length overall: 183.6 in.
      Width: 75.0 in.
      Height: 56.1 in.
      Weight: 3,537 lb

Performance: 0-60: Not known
      Quarter-mile: 12.44 sec. @ 115.08 mph

Production: 50 factory Superstock Ramchargers, 12 with acid-dipped steel bodies. This is the only hardtop sedan built and the only car known sold to a private individual.

Original price: $3,820

1967 Ford Fairlane 500 XL-R 427

First year this engine was offered as Regular Production Option.

Engine: 427 ci from 4.23 in. x 3.78 in.
      425 hp @ 6000 rpm
      480 lb-ft @ 3700 rpm
      11.5:1 compression
      Dual 652 cfm Holley 4V carburetors

Transmission: Ford Top Loader four-speed

Chassis: Wheelbase: 119.0 in.
      Length overall: 197.0 in.
      Width: 74.0 in.
      Height: 51.9 in.
      Weight: 3,350 lb

Performance: 0-60: 6 sec.
      Quarter-mile: 13.8 sec. @ 101 mph

Production: Exact figures not certain, but fewer than 60.

Original price: $4,342

1967 Shelby American AC Cobra 427

Car that began as street version, with engine upgraded to competition specifications. Last year of production.

Engine: Race specifications: Ford V-8, aluminum heads
      427 ci from 4.24 in. x 3.788 in.
      490 bhp @ 6500 rpm
      510 lb-ft @ 3700 rpm
      11.5:1 compression
      Single 780 cfm Holley 4V carburetor

Transmission: Four-speed close-ratio

Chassis: Wheelbase: 90 in.
      Length overall: 156.0 in.
      Width: 70.5 in.
      Height: 49.0 in.
      Weight: 2,150 lb for competition; 2,529 lb in street trim

Performance: 0-60: 3.5 sec.
      0-100-0: 13.8 sec.
      Top speed: 162 mph at 3.31:1 gearing

Production: 356 in street, semi-competition (S/C) and competition specifications.

Original price: $9,750

1967 Plymouth GTX 426 Hemi convertible

First year of production.

Engine: Chrysler hemispherical-headed V-8
      426 ci from 4.25 in. x 3.75 in.
      425 hp @ 5000 rpm
      490 lb-ft @ 4000 rpm
      10.25:1 compression
      Dual Carter AFB 4V carburetors

Transmission: Three-speed automatic

Chassis: Wheelbase: 116.0 in.
      Length overall: 200.5 in.
      Width: 76.4 in.
      Height: 54.1 in.
      Weight: 3,615 lb

Performance: 0-60: 6.3 sec.
      Quarter-mile: 14.0 sec. @ 96.5 mph

Production: 17 total, 7 with four-speeds, 10 with automatics.

Original price: $3,982

1968 Plymouth GTX 426 Hemi convertible

Second year of production. One of 10 remaining.

Engine:	Chrysler hemispherical-headed V-8 426 ci from 4.25 in. x 3.75 in. 425 hp @ 5000 rpm 490 lb-ft @ 4000 rpm 10.25:1 compression Dual Carter AFB 4V carburetors
Transmission:	Heavy-duty four-speed with Hurst linkage
Chassis:	Wheelbase: 116 in. Length overall: 202.7 in. Width: 76.4 in. Height: 54.7 in. Weight: 4,320 lb
Performance:	0-60: 6.1 sec. Quarter-mile: 13.8 sec. @ 101.32 mph
Production:	35; automatic versus four-speed breakdown not known.
Original price:	$4,874

1968 Chevrolet Corvette L-88 convertible

Only roadster known built in International Blue.

Engine:	Chevrolet cast-iron L-88 427 ci from 4.25 in. x 3.75 in. 430 hp @ 5200 rpm 450 lb-ft @ 4400 rpm 12.5:1 compression Single 850 cfm Holley 4V carburetor
Transmission:	Muncie four-speed with Positraction and 4.11 final
Chassis:	Wheelbase: 98.0 in. Length overall: 182.5 in. Width: 69.0 in. Height: 47.9 in. Weight: 3,440 lb

Performance:	0-60: 6.8 sec. Quarter-mile: 13.68 sec. @ 106.89 mph
Production:	80 L-88 Corvettes in 1968.
Original price:	$6,533

1969 Chevrolet Corvette L-88 convertible

The last year for high-compression 427 ci engines.

Engine:	Chevrolet cast-iron L-88 427 ci from 4.25 in. x 3.75 in. 430 hp @ 5200 rpm 450 lb-ft @ 4400 rpm 12.0:1 compression Single 950 cfm Daytona 3V carburetor
Transmission:	Close-ratio four-speed with Positraction limited-slip and 4.11:1 final
Chassis:	Wheelbase: 98.0 in. Length overall: 182.5 in. Width: 69.0 in. Height: 47.8 in. Weight: 3,250 lb
Performance:	0-60: 5.7 sec. Quarter-mile: 13.1 sec. @ 112 mph; 11.5 sec. @ 125 mph in race spec
Production:	116 with the L-88 engine; fewer than 50 were convertibles. Exact production and breakdown of four-speeds versus automatics is not available.
Original price:	$6,400

1968½ Ford Mustang GT Super Cobrajet 428 Ram Air

First year as a Regular Production Option.

Engine:	Ford Super Cobrajet 428 Ram Air 428 ci from 4.13 in. x 3.98 in. 335 hp @ 5600 rpm 445 lb-ft @ 3400 rpm 10.6:1 compression Single 735 cfm Holley 4V carburetor
Transmission:	Ford C-6 three-speed automatic
Chassis:	Wheelbase: 108.0 in. Length overall: 183.6 in. Width: 70.9 in. Height: 51.6 in. Weight: 3,473 lb
Performance:	0-60: 5.9 sec. Quarter-mile: 13.5 sec. @ 106 mph
Production:	Probably fewer than 60 in fastback, notchback and convertible.
Original price:	Not known

1969 Chevrolet Camaro Baldwin Motion Phase III

Most completely optioned Phase III built in 1969.

Engine:	Chevrolet cast-iron L-72 427 ci from 4.25 in. x 3.76 in. 500 hp @ 6500 rpm 535 lb-ft @ 4000 rpm 11.0:1 compression Single 950 cfm Holley 3V carburetor
Transmission:	Muncie M-21 four-speed with Hurst Competition shifter, Positraction limited-slip, Super-bite traction package and 4.56:1 final

1969 Chevrolet Camaro Baldwin Motion Phase III

Chassis:	Wheelbase: 108.1 in.
	Length overall: 184.6 in.
	Width: 72.6 in.
	Height: 51.5 in.
	Weight: 3,303 lb
Performance:	0-60: 4.8 sec.
	Quarter-mile: 11.40 sec. @ 120 mph
Production:	Exact number not certain.
Original price:	$9,330

1969 Chevrolet Corvette Baldwin Motion Phase III

Fewer than 5 exist.

Engine:	Chevrolet cast-iron L-88
	427 ci from 4.25 in. x 3.76 in.
	500 hp @ 6500 rpm
	535 lb-ft @ 4000 rpm
	11.01:1 compression
	Single 950 cfm Holley 3V carburetor
Transmission:	Muncie M-22 Rock Crusher four-speed with Super-bite traction system
Chassis:	Wheelbase: 98.0 in.
	Length overall: 182.5 in.
	Width: 72.0 in.
	Height: 47.8 in.
	Weight: 3,170 lb
Performance:	0-60: 5.4 sec.
	Quarter-mile: 12.35 sec. @ 117 mph
Production:	12.
Original price:	$7,672

1969 Dodge Coronet R/T 426 Hemi convertible

Engine:	Chrysler Hemi V-8
	426 ci from 4.25 in. x 3.75 in.
	425 hp @ 5000 rpm
	490 lb-ft @ 4000 rpm
	10.3:1 compression
	Dual 550 cfm Carter 4V carburetors
Transmission:	Heavy-duty four-speed with Hurst linkage, Sure-Grip limited-slip and 3.54:1 final
Chassis:	Wheelbase: 117.0 in.
	Length overall: 206.7 in.
	Width: 76.7 in.
	Height: 54.0 in.
	Weight: 3,800 lb
Performance:	0-60: 6.7 sec.
	Quarter-mile: 13.85 sec. @ 104 mph
Production:	10; 4 with four-speeds, 6 with automatics. This is currently the only four-speed known to exist.
Original price:	$4,892

1969 Chevrolet Camaro 427 COPO 9561

COPO (Central Office Purchase Order) 9561.

Engine:	Chevrolet cast-iron L-72
	427 ci from 4.25 in. x 3.76 in.
	425 hp @ 5000 rpm
	460 lb-ft @ 4000 rpm
	11.0:1 compression
	Single 780 cfm Holley 4V carburetor
Transmission:	Muncie M-21 close-ratio four-speed with Positraction limited-slip and 4.10:1 final
Chassis:	Wheelbase: 108.1 in.
	Length overall: 186.0 in.
	Width: 74.0 in.
	Height: 51.6 in.
	Weight: 3,400 lb
Performance:	0-60: 4.9 sec.
	Quarter-mile: 12.95 sec. @ 108 mph
Production:	300 in 1969.
Original price:	$4,600

1969 Chevrolet Chevelle Yenko/SC 427

Fewer than 10 of these remain today with the original engine.

Engine:	Chevrolet cast-iron L-72
	427 ci from 4.25 in. x 3.76 in.
	425 hp @ 5000 rpm
	460 lb-ft @ 4000 rpm
	11.0:1 compression
	Single 800 cfm Holley carburetor
Transmission:	Muncie M-40 three-speed automatic with Positraction limited-slip
Chassis:	Wheelbase: 112.0 in.
	Length overall: 197.1 in.
	Width: 75.7 in.
	Height: 51.7 in.
	Weight: 4,100 lb
Performance:	0-60: 5.5 sec.
	Quarter-mile: 11.94 sec. @ 117.95 mph
Production:	99 as factory COPOs; 71 with four-speeds, 28 with automatics.
Original price:	$5,018

1969 Chevrolet Camaro Yenko/SC 427

Approximately 25 Super Yenko Camaros (SCs) exist with complete, original drivetrain.

Engine:
Chevrolet cast-iron L-72
427 ci from 4.25 in. x 3.76 in.
425 hp @ 5000 rpm
460 lb-ft @ 4000 rpm
11.0:1 compression
Single 800 cfm Holley 4V carburetor

Transmission:
Muncie M-40 three-speed automatic with Positraction limited-slip

Chassis:
Wheelbase: 108.1 in.
Length overall: 186.0 in.
Width: 74.0 in.
Height: 51.6 in.
Weight: 3,400 lb

Performance:
0-60: 5.3 sec.
Quarter-mile: 13.05 sec. @ 105.5 mph

Production:
201 total; 171 with Muncie M-21 four-speeds, 30 with automatics.

Original price: $5,200

1969 Dodge Charger Daytona 426 Hemi

At present, only 11 Hemi-engined four-speed cars exist.

Engine:
Chrysler hemispherical-head V-8
426 ci from 4.25 in. x 3.75 in.
425 hp @ 5000 rpm
490 lb-ft @ 4000 rpm
10.3:1 compression
Dual 550 cfm Carter 4V carburetors

Transmission:
Heavy-duty four-speed with Hurst linkage, Sure-Grip limited-slip and 3.54:1 final

Chassis:
Wheelbase: 117.0 in.
Length overall: 226.5 in.
Width: 76.6 in.
Height: 53.0 in. to top of wing
Weight: 4,151 lb

Performance:
0-60: 6.7 sec.
Quarter-mile: 13.9 sec. @ 101 mph

Production:
500 to qualify as a production car for NASCAR racing; 70 with the Hemi engine, 22 with four-speeds, 48 with automatics.

Original price: $5,342

1969 Chevrolet Camaro Z-28 302 Cross Ram

Street version of Sports Car Club of America Trans-Am racing series entry, produced to homologate car for competition.

Engine:
Chevrolet cast-iron Z-28
302 ci from 4.00 in. x 3.00 in.
290 hp @ 5800 rpm
290 lb-ft @ 4200 rpm
11.0:1 compression
Dual 600 cfm Holley 4V carburetors and Cross Ram induction

Transmission:
Muncie M-21 four-speed with Positraction limited-slip and 4.10:1 final

Chassis:
Wheelbase: 108.1 in.
Length overall: 186.0 in.
Width: 74.0 in.
Height: 51.6 in.
Weight: 3,455 lb

Performance:
0-60: 7.4 sec.
Quarter-mile: 15.12 sec. @ 94.8 mph

Production:
206 including cars from Roger Penske Sunoco racing team.

Original price: $5,207

1969 Chevrolet Corvette ZL-1 427

Originally produced for drag strip use.

Engine:
Chevrolet cast aluminum
427 ci from 4.25 in. x 3.76 in.
430 hp @ 5800 rpm
460 lb-ft @ 4000 rpm
12.5:1 compression
Single 850 cfm Holley 4V carburetor
(All specifications for street exhaust.)

Transmission:
Muncie M-22 Rock Crusher four-speed

Chassis:
Wheelbase: 98.0 in.
Length overall: 182.5 in.
Width: 69.0 in.
Height: 47.9 in.
Weight: 3,150 lb

Performance:
0-60: 5.2 sec.
Quarter-mile: 13.5 sec. @ 111.5 mph

Production:
3 Corvettes with the ZL-1 engine were built, 2 were offered to the public. Both still exist. The third, a development car, was destroyed by Chevrolet.

Original price: $10,319

1969 Chevrolet Camaro ZL-1 427 COPO 9560

COPO 9560, originally produced for National Hot Rod Association Super/Stock drag racing. Approximately 32 remain, though only 5 retain their original all-aluminum engine.

Engine:
Chevrolet cast aluminum
427 ci from 4.25 in. x 3.76 in.
430 hp @ 5600 rpm
450 lb-ft @ 4400 rpm
12.5:1 compression

1969 Chevrolet Camaro ZL-1 427 COPO 9560

Single 850 cfm Holley 4V carburetor
(All specifications for street exhaust.)

Transmission: Muncie M-21 four-speed with Positraction limited-slip and 4.10:1 final
Chassis: Wheelbase: 108.1 in.
Length overall: 186.0 in.
Width: 74.0 in.
Height: 51.6 in.
Weight: 3,288 lb
Performance: 0-60: 5.2 sec.
Quarter-mile: 13.16 sec. @ 119.06 mph
Production: 69; 47 with M-21 four-speed, 22 with automatic transmissions.
Original price: $7,702

1970 Buick Gran Sport GSX Stage I 455

Engine: 455 ci from 4.31 in. x 3.90 in.
360 hp @ 4600 rpm
510 lb-ft @ 2800 rpm
10.1:1 compression
Single 780 cfm Rochester Quadrajet carburetor
Transmission: Three-speed Turbo Hydra-matic with Positraction limited-slip and 3.64:1 final
Chassis: Wheelbase: 112.0 in.
Length overall: 200.7 in.
Width: 75.6 in.
Height: 53.4 in.
Weight: 3,908 lb
Performance: 0-60: 6.4 sec.
Quarter-mile: 13.95 sec. @ 100.5 mph
Production: 678; 479 in yellow, 199 in white. All were coupes.
Original price: $5,479

1970 Chevrolet Chevelle SS Baldwin Motion Phase III 454

Engine: LS-6
454 ci from 4.25 in. x 4.00 in.
500 hp @ 6500 rpm
500 lb-ft @ 4800 rpm
11.0:1 compression
Single 780 cfm Holley 4V carburetor
Transmission: Muncie M-22 four-speed with Hurst Competition shifter, Positraction limited-slip, Hone-A-Drive, 4.88:1 final and 3.70:1 overdrive
Chassis: Wheelbase: 112.0 in.
Length overall: 197.2 in.
Width: 75.6 in.
Height: 52.6 in.
Weight: 3,885 lb
Performance: 0-60: 4.4 sec.
Quarter-mile: 12.0 sec. @ 118 mph
Production: Fewer than 12 built.
Original price: $8,010

1970 Dodge Challenger T/A 340 Six-Pack

Produced by Dodge to qualify for Sports Car Club of America's Trans-Am race series.

Engine: Dodge 340 Six-Pack V-8
340 ci from 4.04 in. x 3.31 in.
290 hp @ 5000 rpm
345 lb-ft @ 3400 rpm
10.5:1 compression
Triple Holley 2V carburetors for 1150 cfm total
Transmission: Chrysler close-ratio four-speed with Hurst linkage, Sure-Grip limited-slip and 3.55:1 final

Chassis: Wheelbase: 110.0 in.
Length overall: 191.3 in.
Width: 76.1 in.
Height: 50.6 in.
Weight: 3,390 lb
Performance: 0-60: 5.8 sec.
Quarter-mile: 14.3 sec. @ 99.5 mph
Production: About 2,700, with both four-speed and automatic versions. No breakdown is available.
Original price: $4,074

1970 Dodge Coronet R/T 426 Hemi convertible

The last year Dodge produced a full-size convertible.

Engine: Dodge hemispherical-head V-8
426 ci from 4.25 in. x 3.75 in.
425 hp @ 5000 rpm
490 lb-ft @ 4000 rpm
10.25:1 compression
Dual 550 cfm Carter 4V carburetors
Transmission: Four-speed manual with Super Track Pak, limited-slip and 4.10:1 final
Chassis: Wheelbase: 117.0 in.
Length overall: 209.2 in.
Width: 76.7 in.
Height: 54.1 in.
Weight: 3,600 lb
Performance: 0-60: 6.7 sec.
Quarter-mile: 13.90 sec. @ 105 mph
Production: According to Chrysler records, only 2 Coronet Hemi convertibles were built, both with four-speeds. The other was reported destroyed by fire.
Original price: $6,160

1970 Oldsmobile 4-4-2 W-30 455 convertible

The first production year for the W-30 package with cold air induction.

Engine:	455 ci from 4.12 in. x 4.25 in. 370 hp @ 5200 rpm 500 lb-ft @ 3600 rpm 10.5:1 compression Single Rochester 4V carburetor
Transmission:	Three-speed Turbo Hydra-matic with Hurst Sport shifter linkage, Positraction limited-slip and 3.55:1 final
Chassis:	Wheelbase: 112.0 in. Length overall: 203.2 in. Width: 76.2 in. Height: 52.8 in. Weight; 3,887 lb
Performance:	0-60: 6.8 sec. Quarter-mile: 14.2 sec. @ 102.14 mph
Production:	264.
Original price:	$4,480

1970 Pontiac GTO Judge 400 Ram Air IV convertible

Engine:	Pontiac 400 Ram Air IV 400 ci from 4.12 in. x 3.746 in. 366 hp @ 5100 rpm 445 lb-ft @ 3600 rpm 10.5:1 compression Single Rochester 4V carburetor
Transmission:	Three-speed Turbo Hydra-matic with Positraction limited-slip and 3.55:1 final
Chassis:	Wheelbase: 112.0 in. Length overall: 202.9 in. Width: 76.7 in.

	Height: 52.3 in. Weight: 4,055 lb
Performance:	0-60: 6.6 sec. Quarter-mile: 14.6 sec. @ 99.55 mph
Production:	168; breakdown between four-speeds and automatics is not known.
Original price:	$5,864

1970 Plymouth 'Cuda 426 Hemi Pink Panther

Believed to be the only Pink Panther Barracuda left in existence.

Engine:	Plymouth hemispherical-head V-8 426 ci from 4.25 in. x 3.75 in. 425 hp @ 5000 rpm 490 lb-ft @ 4000 rpm 10.25:1 compression Dual 550 cfm Carter 4V carburetors
Transmission:	TorqueFlite three-speed automatic with Sure-Grip limited-slip and 4.10:1 final
Chassis:	Wheelbase: 108.0 in. Length overall: 186.6 in. Width: 74.7 in. Height: 50.0 in. Weight: 3,750 lb
Performance:	0-60: 5.8 sec. Quarter-mile: 13.95 sec. @ 105 mph
Production:	Approximately 736; 325 with four-speeds, 411 with TorqueFlites.
Original price:	$4,700

1971 Plymouth 'Cuda 426 Hemi

Currently has 526 miles, one of the lowest mileages known.

Engine:	Plymouth hemispherical-head V-8 426 ci from 4.25 in. x 3.75 in. 425 hp @ 5000 rpm 490 lb-ft @ 4000 rpm 10.2:1 compression Dual 550 cfm Carter 4V carburetors
Transmission:	TorqueFlite High-Upshift three-speed automatic with Sure-Grip limited-slip and 4.10:1 final
Chassis:	Wheelbase: 108.0 in. Length overall: 186.6 in. Width: 74.7 in. Height: 51.9 in. Weight: 3,400 lb
Performance:	0-60: 5.3 sec. Quarter-mile: 13.56 sec. @ 105 mph
Production:	108; 48 with four-speeds, 60 with automatics.
Original price:	$4,640

1970 Plymouth 'Cuda 426 Hemi convertible

Believed to be the only green Hemi 'Cuda convertible ever built.

Engine:	Plymouth hemispherical-head V-8 426 ci from 4.25 in. x 3.75 in. 425 hp @ 5000 rpm 490 lb-ft @ 4000 rpm 10.25:1 compression Dual 550 cfm Carter 4V carburetors

1970 Plymouth 'Cuda 426 Hemi convertible

Transmission: TorqueFlite three-speed automatic with Sure-Grip limited-slip and 3.55:1 final

Chassis: Wheelbase: 108.0 in.
Length overall: 186.6 in.
Width: 74.7 in.
Height: 51.9 in.
Weight: 3,800 lb

Performance: 0–60: 6.0 sec.
Quarter-mile: 13.5 sec. @ 104.5 mph

Production: 14; 6 with four-speeds, 8 with automatics.

Original price: $5,200

1970 Dodge Challenger R/T 426 Hemi convertible

Engine: Dodge hemispherical-head V-8 426 ci from 4.25 in. x 3.75 in.
425 hp @ 5000 rpm
490 lb-ft @ 4000 rpm
10.2:1 compression
Dual 550 cfm Carter 4V carburetors

Transmission: TorqueFlite three-speed automatic with Sure-Grip limited-slip and 3.55:1 final

Chassis: Wheelbase: 110.0 in.
Length overall: 191.3 in.
Width: 76.1 in.
Height: 50.6 in.
Weight: 3,890 lb

Performance: 0–60: 5.8 sec.
Quarter-mile: 14.1 sec. @ 103.2 mph

Production: 9; 5 with four-speeds, 4 with automatics. 7 survive.

Original price: $5,200

1971 Dodge Challenger R/T 426 Hemi

Engine: Dodge hemispherical-head V-8 426 ci from 4.25 in. x 3.75 in.
425 hp @ 5000 rpm
490 lb-ft @ 4000 rpm
10.2:1 compression
Dual 550 cfm Carter 4V carburetors

Transmission: Four-speed manual with Sure-Grip limited-slip and 4.10:1 final

Chassis: Wheelbase: 110.0 in.
Length overall: 191.3 in.
Width: 76.1 in.
Height: 50.6 in.
Weight: 3,700 lb

Performance: 0–60: 6.0 sec.
Quarter-mile: 13.70 sec. @ 105 mph

Production: 71; 59 with four-speeds, 12 with automatics.

Original price: $4,992

1971 Dodge Charger R/T 426 Hemi

Believed to be the only triple-black Hemi Charger built.

Engine: Dodge hemispherical-head V-8 426 ci from 4.25 in. x 3.75 in.
425 hp @ 5000 rpm
490 lb-ft @ 4000 rpm
10.2:1 compression
Dual 550 cfm Carter 4V carburetors

Transmission: TorqueFlite three-speed automatic with 3.54:1 final

Chassis: Wheelbase: 115.0 in.
Length overall: 205.4 in.
Width: 79.1 in.
Height: 52.2 in.
Weight: 4,050 lb

Performance: 0–60: 6.0 sec.
Quarter-mile: 14.15 sec. @ 103 mph

Production: 63; 30 with four-speeds, 33 with TorqueFlites.

Original price: $4,500

1971 Dodge Charger Super Bee 426 Hemi

Fewer than 10 are known to exist.

Engine: Dodge hemispherical-head V-8 426 ci from 4.25 in. x 3.75 in.
425 hp @ 5000 rpm
490 lb-ft @ 4000 rpm
10.2:1 compression
Dual 550 cfm Carter 4V carburetors

Transmission: TorqueFlite three-speed automatic with Sure-Grip limited-slip and 3.54:1 final

Chassis: Wheelbase: 115.0 in.
Length overall: 205.4 in.
Width: 79.1 in.
Height: 52.0 in.
Weight: 4,083 lb

Performance: 0–60: 5.7 sec.
Quarter-mile: 13.73 sec. @ 104 mph

Production: 22; 9 with four-speeds, 13 with automatics.

Original price: $4,600